Easy-to-learn finance practices for entrepreneurs who want to achieve high performance

WHAT THE FINANCE

SANGEETA SHANKARAN SUMESH

INDIA • SINGAPORE • MALAYSIA

Notion Press

Old No. 38, New No. 6
McNichols Road, Chetpet
Chennai - 600 031

First Published by Notion Press 2019
Copyright © Sangeeta Shankaran Sumesh 2019
Red Brick Green Back Consulting
All Rights Reserved.

ISBN 978-1-64546-796-0

This book has been published with all efforts taken to make the material error-free after the consent of the author. However, the author and the publisher do not assume and hereby disclaim any liability to any party for any loss, damage, or disruption caused by errors or omissions, whether such errors or omissions result from negligence, accident, or any other cause.

No part of this book may be used, reproduced in any manner whatsoever without written permission from the author, except in the case of brief quotations embodied in critical articles and reviews.

This book is dedicated to all entrepreneurs,
intrapreneurs and business heads,
who want to enhance their business performance.

Contents

What the Author Has to Say   7
Gratitude   11

Chapter 1: What You Should Start With   15
Chapter 2: What You Can Do   31
Chapter 3: What Will Keep You Going   47
Chapter 4: What Is Your Spend   69
Chapter 5: What Is In Your Bank   110
Chapter 6: What To Watch Out For   127
Chapter 7: What Is Your Why   138
Chapter 8: What Will Take You Further   161
Chapter 9: What Is Your Inspiration   180
Chapter 10: What You Need To Know   234

WHAT THE AUTHOR HAS TO SAY

Why Read This Book?
- "How will I pay next month's salaries?"
- "How can I get [more] funding?"
- "How are some entrepreneurs so successful in financial terms?"
- "What are the meanings of the financial terms my investors keep referring to?"
- "What is 'financial management' all about?"
- "How can I grow my profits further?"
- "How can I get to know what I need to do to manage my business's finances?"

The above-mentioned are some of the common concerns raised by many entrepreneurs. It is indicative of their relative lack of knowledge about core financial concepts and, correspondingly, their superficial understanding of finance-related issues—both of which have a direct bearing on their business operations. Put two and two together, and we find evidence for the oft-mentioned fact that many businesses fail due to poor financial management.

As a finance professional with over two decades of experience in financial management, I aim to make the lives of entrepreneurs/intrapreneurs easier by simplifying matters related to finance. This, I hope, will enable better understanding and help them make effective financial business decisions.

What the Author Has to Say

As an entrepreneur, you may have great business ideas but handling the finances of your business may not be your cup of tea. As your business grows, you realise that making profits is harder than expected (or believed). While revenue may be on a positive climb, making profits could be elusive. In order to succeed, you need to focus on your revenue, keep a tab on your costs *and* allow profits to be the driver of your business. Profits reflect the health of the business, and are required for better valuation of the business.

Thus, one of the key objectives of any business is to maximise profits. While it is well known that the difference between revenue and costs results in profits (or loss), the primary goal of a business is to be profitable and ensure sustainability. Profit is the core of any business—irrespective of the industry it pertains to. One might even say that profit is the very basis of the existence of a business.

Over my career, I have noticed that, while most entrepreneurs/business owners are extremely passionate about their product or service, they seem to face several problems when it comes to managing their business's finances. This is a common issue in the start-up community, as budding entrepreneurs (sometimes) lack experience as entrepreneurs and/or are not familiar with handling financial matters.

The more I interacted with entrepreneurs, the greater the realisation that there was a common thread running amongst them, irrespective of the nature, size and type of industry they were dealing in: *The challenge of handling the finances of their business.* They found it too complex, too cumbersome, or downright boring—if not, they lacked passion in handling the financial aspects pertaining to their entity. As a Finance Professional and a High Performance Coach, I felt that the best I could do to help this community was to simplify the subject of finance and provide some practical tips that would help them take greater strides towards the ultimate objective of maximising profits.

What Is This Book All About?

Given the above, I felt the need to demystify the subject of finance for entrepreneurs who find it daunting—as if it were the sword of Damocles hanging over them. As there are already a number of academic books on understanding finance and its concepts, I am not going to explain the concepts or the terms in depth. I am looking at making the subject simple and easier to grasp, with a focus on practical matters, and to present this book as a guide not only to young entrepreneurs but also to entrepreneurs who want to scale up to the next level. The ultimate objective of writing this book is to steer entrepreneurs towards utilising the full performance potential of their business, so as to maximise their profits.

Therefore, I am providing basic and simple ways by which profits can be maximised. I have also given some 'points for reflection' at the end of most topics for entrepreneurs to ponder and think about points for reflection. This would aid a self-driven evaluation of their business and thereby trigger better performance.

I have also spiced up this book with the real-life, inspirational financial journeys of some successful entrepreneurs, who have shared their financial challenges, learnings and words of wisdom for the upcoming generation of entrepreneurs.

What Can You Gain From This Book?

How can profits grow? What are the ways and means through which a business can be made profitable? How can profits be maximised? This book touches on some simple steps that can be followed to maximise profits, irrespective of the business you are in. They are:

1. Enhancing revenue
2. Controlling costs
3. Adhering to applicable compliances
4. Maintaining financial discipline
5. Following best practices

Based on the above, I have sub-divided the above categories into smaller topics, which will act as pointers, and provided some suggestions on enhancing profits as well. Before delving into them further, I have also given some general best practices that can be followed, which will enable better financial discipline.

In the last section, I am also giving a gist of the financial journey of few successful entrepreneurs who have been there and done that. By reading these real-life lessons, you can avoid committing the same financial mistakes as them, and even learn some valuable lessons from their experience. These entrepreneurs have been kind enough to share the challenges that they encountered, what worked well for them, what did not and so on. They have further supplemented it with what they have learnt over time.

How To Read This Book?

Here are some suggestions on how you can read this book.

- If you are not so familiar with basic financial terms, I suggest you first read Chapter 10 of this book, as it provides a simple reference for some of the commonly used financial terms. Of course, feel free to refer to it at any point in time as well.
- I am taking you through the business of a fictitious entity—SRI Ventures, started by Sid, Ram and Isha. You may open the book and read any of the sub-section of each chapter, as per your preference. It is not necessary to the follow the sequence of the book, as each of the topics is independent of the other.
- Read the topics that are applicable to your business and, if you want, feel free to skip the rest. If you feel you already know the topic, feel free to move on to the next topic.
- Think about how you can use the reflections (at the end of each sub-section) to raise your business performance.

What Do I Wish For?

What I would like is for your business profits to grow. More so, I would be glad if this book is of help in enabling you to understand finance better, assist you in managing money matters more efficiently, and aid you in making the right business decisions—which, in turn, will pave the way for higher profits.

My best wishes to all the entrepreneurs and intrapreneurs reading this book. May you maximise your knowledge about finance and may your profits grow in leaps and bounds.

Sangeeta Shankaran Sumesh

GRATITUDE

With a grateful heart, I would like to acknowledge the following people who have contributed to the shaping of this book:

- After my first book, *A Glance at the Unknown*, was published, many people told me to write a finance book. Among them, I would specially want to thank friends Naveen Valsakumar, Pravin Shekar, Panneerselvam Madanagopal and Premkumar Rajmohan who motivated me to start writing, this book.
- All the wonderful entrepreneurs featured in Chapter 9 of this book, who contributed to a very great extent. They spent their time and energy and shared their finance journeys, challenges and learnings, which would be very useful for budding entrepreneurs. A big thanks from the bottom of my heart to:
    - Arun Jain, Intellect Design Arena
    - Arokiasamy Velumani, Thyrocare
    - Badri Seshadri, Cricinfo.com
    - C.K. Kumaravel, Naturals Spa & Salon
    - Girish Mathrubootham, Freshworks Inc
    - Harish Suri, Arknemesis Gaming & Café
    - Rajesh Parthasarathy, Mentis Software
    - Murugavel Janakiraman, Matrimony.com
    - M.V. Subramanian, Future Focus Infotech

GRATITUDE

- Naveen Valsakumar, Notion Press
- Prabhakaran Murugaiah, Techfetch.com
- Ranjani Manian, Global Adjustments
- Suresh Sambandam, OrangeScape
- Suresh Shankar, Crayon data
- Umesh Sachdev, Uniphore Software Systems

- Thank you to the following angel investors who shared their perspectives on what they expect.
  - Rajan Anandan, Managing Director, Google India
  - V. Shankar, Founder, Computer Age Management Services (CAMS) Private Limited

- Heartfelt thanks to the following entrepreneurs who spoke to me in detail regarding their business struggles, especially from the finance perspective
  - Surendranath Reddy, Founder, Redd
  - Bhanu Murugan, Founder, Access Teq Systems
  - Sujata Tarakesan, Founder, Chennaigaga
  - Arvind Narayanan, Founder TechAgro
  - Adithya Narayanan, Founder and Director, Cryptic Intel
  - Vikram Chintalapati, Swagene
  - Ashwin Chandran, Founder, Ideas Inc.
  - Arunachalam Venkat, Kamalam Builders
  - Srihari S., CAE Consultants
  - Anush Rajasekaran, Co-Founder, Mezze
  - Mukesh Devanathan, Codum Technologies
  - Hiren Barai, Partner, Commutatus
  - Tamilselvan Mahalingam, Founder, Future Captains
  - Komandur Srinivasan, Managing Director, Chakrath Consultants
  - Arthi Alwar, Associate, MTA Architects
  - Manu Sekar, Founder and CEO, TechDiva

- My children – Shrey & Svara for putting up with my writing phase over the weekends and holidays. My chartered accountant

husband, Sumesh, for being a beta editor. My mother, Sukanya Shankar, for all her encouragement and support.
- Thank you to my chartered accountant friends for their technical evaluation of the book.
  - P. C. Balasubramanian, Founder, ED & President, Matrix Business Services
  - Lakshmi N.P., Partner, L N P & Associates
  - Srinivasa Chary, Manager, Dun & Bradstreet Technologies
  - Aswin Vaidyanathan, Partner, Grant Thornton
- The entire Notion Press team for the amazing cover design, editing and efficient delivery.
- Special thanks to Kabir Chandra for the picture on the cover.

Chapter 1

WHAT YOU SHOULD START WITH

It is not just you who is confused, and wondering about what, where and how to go about getting a hang of your business's finances. Even the most successful entrepreneurs have had their share of nightmares when it comes to handling finance. The good news is, once you know how to tackle it, you become a master.

Each business has desired growth objectives. What are the right elements required to accomplish them from a financial perspective? How can you go about achieving them with ease?

You don't have to reinvent the wheel, as the answers to these questions have been found out, and tried and tested over the years. Certain business processes and practices have emerged successful, and are considered healthy—and, therefore, worthy of adoption. Also known as 'financial best practices', they are reliable, help in managing risk and drive business value.

A 'best practice' refers to the process of utilising proven practices, concepts and strategies from other organisations with similar operations or in similar industries. Adopting best practices helps in improving performance in specific, targeted areas, which thereby results in better process, controls and profits. It helps generate financial savings, enhances operational efficiencies and ensures that the same mistakes are not repeated.

There might not be just a single best way to accomplish a task. Similarly, there are several best practices across industries. Some of the healthy financial best practices, which will help a business to lay a good foundation, are highlighted here. These best practices can then be customised according to the industry standards and improvised specifically for each individual business based on the internal working culture, processes and respective working styles.

If you are already running your own business, evaluate which of the best practices you have already implemented and which ones you would like to include. If you are a new entrepreneur, you can incorporate all of these best practices.

I have classified the practices into various sub-topics for easy reading, and for providing you with some thoughts for your action(s) after each topic.

Financial Goals

Have you thought about the following?

- What is the purpose of your business?
- What is your drive to run your business?
- What are your financial objectives?
- Have you quantified your financial objectives?

Without having specific goals, you will lack direction and end up groping in the dark. So, it is important to set your financial goals and keep tab of them.

> Take the case of SRI Ventures, which was started by Sid, Ram and Isha. They wanted to grow their business—by which they meant doubling their revenue. When further probed if they had any specific internal target to be achieved in terms of profit, they admitted that they were undecided. They claimed that their business was in a nascent stage, and that they were expecting losses, and intending to break-even in subsequent years. Are you thinking on similar lines? While it may be good to be mentally prepared for losses in the initial stages, it is wise to set a specific time period for growth of the margins. This will be a target towards which growth can be propelled.

Note that growth in revenue need not necessarily mean that your profits are growing as well. Even after reaching the break-even point and ensuring the onset of profits, it is vital to remain self-sustaining for the years ahead and grow your profits year on year. It is also important to measure the growth in terms of revenue, margins, return on capital employed, margin per employee and so on.

Apart from wanting to double their revenue, SRI did not have any other financial goals. What were they missing? Financial goals could also include maximising market share, buying specific equipment, having a certain amount as reserves, zero debt and so on.

Financial goals can be specified for each time period. Therefore, it is good to have short-term, medium-term and long-term financial goals, and plan the business' strategies around the same. Thus, it is crucial to set the right financial goals, which will provide clarity and propel your business towards the set objectives.

Effective financial goals for your business may be set by focusing on increasing revenue, decreasing costs, moving towards better gross margins, effective cash management, higher profit per employee and so on, and thereby striving for financial success. Goals should be forward-looking. Therefore, derive the steps that need to be taken in working towards your desired goals.

> **Reflections:**
> - *What are the short-term, medium-term and long-term financial goals for your business?*
> - *List your financial goals for each period with specific details (in terms of revenue, margins, manpower and other relevant parameters)*
> - *What is the plan you have laid out to achieve the above goals?*

Business Plan

While there is no legal mandate that requires a business plan, it is necessary to have one, as it acts as your sounding board to measure progress and as a pointer for the way forward. It is a roadmap that states your business goals, where your business would be heading in the coming years and how your business will work towards achieving it. It is a blueprint of the actions that are required to be taken.

A business plan assists in formulating strategy, helps in understanding the market, validates the feasibility of the project, aids in raising funds, and provides clarity in the SWOT (Strength, Weakness, Opportunities and Threat) analysis of the business. Hence, it is a good practice to have a business plan in place right at the start of the business, and update it at periodic intervals. The plan also serves as an essential document to convince bankers and helps support your funding requirements.

> Let's look at SRI again. All three of them wanted to grow their revenue. However, Sid was thinking of revenue growth by increasing the number of customers, Ram was thinking about increasing their prices, and Isha wanted to start a new vertical. Thus, their individual energies were not fully in sync with each other. By not having a business plan in place, the three of them were not aligned in their thinking. Each of them had different visions and strategies to achieve the revenue growth and all in their head.
>
> When SRI was asked to prepare a business plan by their potential investor, the trio realised their differences in thinking. By sitting together and discussing, they managed to collate their ideas together and work towards a unified strategy to achieve their goals.

Do you have your business plans clearly spelt out?

Some of the key elements that should be part of your business plan are:

- Executive summary (what you expect your business to accomplish).
- Business description (key information about your business, such as vision, mission, nature of operations, your goals and so on).
- Target market (market expectations and how your business will fit in).
- Competitor analysis (your edge against your direct and indirect competitors).

- Details about your offerings (your product/services, value proposition and so on).
- Business model (revenue generation, expected margins, financial metrics and so on).
- Marketing plan (strategy to reach your potential clients).
- Sales strategy (the plan to sell, sales targets and so on).
- Financial projections (P&L or profit and loss forecast for the next 3 to 5 years, with the basis of preparation).
- Request for funding (amount required, and the plan for utilisation of the funds).

The business plan should be simple, straightforward and practical in terms of adhering to and achieving the stated goals and objectives. The entrepreneur can create a business plan and sow the seeds of growth around it.

> Reflections:
> - *Create your business plan.*
> - *If there is one in place, list the actual deviations and gaps (as you observed them) from the business plan. What steps can be taken to improvise and bring your business back on track?*
> - *How often do you review and update your business plan?*

Budget

You must be already aware that a budget is an estimate of income and expenses for a particular period of time. All the known and anticipated revenue (based on estimated sales volumes) and anticipated expenses are slotted into the P&L (profit and loss account). This reflects the financial status of the business's planned operations. The budget can be made as detailed as possible, and reflect the performance of each individual line item on the P&L. Having a budget makes it easy for you to track your progress.

> Why is it important to have a budget in place? In the case of SRI, they had an overall budget to achieve a profit margin of 5 per cent but had failed to list it down specifically. So, they were in a dilemma of not knowing how much to spend on each expense item. They lacked clarity on what could be the maximum spend on salaries or how much they could stretch their marketing expense. The three of them had set a revenue target together but they were not sure about the rest of the P&L line items. What is the case with you?

Apart from the budgeted P&L, you can also prepare a cash flow budget based on the cash requirements of the business. Further, a projected balance sheet may also be drawn, based on the capital investments on assets, liabilities and equity.

Budgets act as financial guides and help in measuring the business's actual financial performance. Unfavourable deviations from the budget must be scrutinised, and efforts must be made right away to get back on track, in line with the budget.

> Reflections:
> - *What are the best- and worse-case scenarios that your budget reveals about your business?*
> - *List the line items where the budget has not been met. Analyse the deviations.*
> - *Going forward, how can you ensure the actual expenses do not exceed the budgeted amounts?*

Policies And Procedures

Policies and procedures are intended to specify the boundaries of your business activities. They help to regulate business operations, and aid in decision-making and efficient management of business. It is best to have policies and procedures documented, and update them periodically in line with the growth of the business.

The business's policies must specify the framework on how to deal with challenges and ensure that business operations are carried out in a fair and consistent manner within the entity. Some essential policies you can have are leave policy, travel policy, information security policy, whistle blower policy, HR policy and so on.

> In our example of SRI, one of the employees had undertaken a three-day business trip. Upon returning, he submitted a reimbursement claim. The employee felt he had adhered to the travel policy, and was expecting all the expenses he had incurred to be reimbursed. However, the claim also included liquor bills. As per SRI's existing travel policy, all business-related travel and accommodation were to be reimbursed, but nothing was mentioned about liquor bills. The employee was under the impression that this amount was be reimbursed, as it was a business trip. The employer, on the other hand, was not planning to pay for the liquor bills as he felt this expense was personal in nature. The travel policy did not state anything about liquor bills, thus making it a grey area. So, SRI realised that it was essential for policies to clearly state the rules that were to set the stage for business operations.

Procedure is a documented description of prescribed course(s) of action or process(es) to enable adherence to the business's policies. It details the path to be taken to execute a task. Examples of procedures include purchase procedure, invoicing procedure, payroll procedure and so on, which reveal the step-by-step action to be performed towards the desired result.

It is important for you to have well-laid and documented policies and procedures, as they will assist you in having better internal control within the organisation.

> **Reflections:**
> - *When was the last time you reviewed the policies and procedures of your business?*
> - *How are you monitoring the effectiveness of the above?*
> - *What happens if the team does not comply with the stated policies and procedures?*

Cash Management

You would agree that cash is a crucial component for any business activity. Cash is essential to make all the required payments to employees, vendors, regulators and so on. For cash outflow to take place effectively, you have to ensure that cash inflow occurs without any hitches. The timing of the requirement of cash in and cash out has to be planned meticulously. Cash management is also known as treasury management.

> In SRI, month after month, the trio had nightmares before each payroll cycle. Sometimes, the salaries were paid after a few days' delay, which gave their employees a feeling of insecurity. While they gave importance to all their vendors and paid them on time, they were unsure of when their customers were going to pay them. They were not aggressive enough in following up on their dues. Further, they did not have a clue about non-routine payments, which led to mismanagement of cash and delayed payment of salaries.

How effectively are you managing your cash? Do you think it is important?

Effective cash management ensures that the business is enduring well and is financial stable, and that the entity is solvent. It is your responsibility to safeguard the cash that belongs to the business. This involves efficient collection, handling and proper usage of the cash.

The objective of cash management is to maximise liquidity and control cash flow. It is good to have a positive cash balance as it enables settling of dues, reinvestment in the business, returning of money to shareholders and acting as a buffer for future unforeseen financial challenges, and so on.

> **Reflections:**
> - *What system(s) do you have in place to monitor your cash situation?*
> - *How frequently do you review your cash balance?*
> - *Quantify the cash reserves of your business so as to know how long your business can sustain independently.*

Accounting Software

There are several readymade accounting software in the market. With the introduction of cloud accounting solutions (like Zoho Books: https://www.zoho.com/books), businesses are able to manage their finances, automate their workflow, stay tax compliant and access their data from anywhere.

Opting for a cloud accounting solution can also help your business to collaborate with the accountant and colleagues better. You can choose a software that connects the front office and back office so that you can reduce data entry and the errors associated with it.

While it is not mandatory to have accounting software, it is always beneficial to have an accounting software implemented, more so because all your business transactions are captured in one particular place.

> When SRI started their business, they were maintaining their bills, invoices and receipts in a file. At the end of each quarter, the data was given to their accountant for maintaining their books. They were not tracking their expenses or their financial position. As their initial operations were small, they were able to keep track of the expenses easily. However, as SRI started to grow, they were finding it difficult to manage, and they decided to choose an accounting software that would also generate financial reports.

They concluded that an integrated software would be ideal as it would encompass all necessary aspects – from incurring an expense to settling it, as well as generating an invoice. It would track the invoice until payment was collected as well. Further, the accounting software could generate financial statements (P&L statement and balance sheet) of the business, which would help in evaluating the business's financial progress over a specified period of time.

Accounting software further aids in performing bank reconciliations, maintaining a history of transactions, providing an audit trail, generating various reports and so on. Accounting software also comes integrated with banking solutions. Based on your requirements, chose the most appropriate accounting software.

> **Reflections:**
> - *When was the last time you upgraded your business accounting software?*
> - *How frequently do you back up the data in your software?*
> - *What are the access levels given to the teams for using the software?*

Cost Control vs. Cost Reduction

As the name suggests, cost control refers to regulating, supervising and guiding the costs whereas cost reduction refers to decreasing the costs.

> To give you an example, let us look at SRI's travel costs. Controlling travel costs implies the need to take a decision as to whether incurring a particular travel cost is necessary or not. This will be further validated by a cost–benefit analysis: *Does the benefit of undertaking the travel outweigh the cost that will be incurred for the particular travel?* SRI concluded that not all travel/trips are required. For instance, their meeting with an overseas customer was completed via e-conferencing facility, thereby ensuring that travel costs were controlled.

Usually, cost control can be implemented on avoidable costs. However, it is to be decided on a case-to-case basis.

Reduction of travel costs can relate to reducing overall travel expenses. SRI decided that there can be a reduction in the levels of travel allowance, and went on to redefine the organisation's travel policy of the organisation (Ex: Explicit condition of travelling by economy class vis-à-vis business class).

Cost reduction can be implemented on non-avoidable costs, such as negotiating for a better price. Thus, you need to take effective decisions for each line item under costs and ensure that, while the costs are kept at a minimum, the business operations are not affected. Also, note that while making decisions, long-term impact on the business should also be taken into account.

> **Reflections:**
> - *Identify key levers for cost reduction.*
> - *Explore possible areas of cost control and cost reduction.*
> - *What can you do differently in each of the above identified areas with regard to cost control and cost reduction?*

Audit

> At SRI, in order to save costs, the trio initially decided not to appoint auditors. Furthermore, they felt that, since they were friends, they trusted each other when it came to money matters. However, pretty soon, they changed their minds, as their mentor advised them on the importance of getting their books audited (highlighted below).

Audits are necessary costs for your organisation, as they keep a tab on not only the finance of your organisation but also on compliances, efficiency, frauds and so on. An audit also provides comfort to your investors by assuring them that the money they invested is spent prudently. There are different types of audits—such as statutory audit, internal audit, tax audit, due diligence audit and so on. The income tax department and other regulators also seek the audited financial statements, as they rely on the same.

A statutory audit is undertaken by external auditors (practising chartered accountants). Internal audits are conducted by internal auditors, who could be either employees of the company or consultants from audit firms. Internal audits are mandatory only for companies with turnover above a certain threshold. Otherwise, it is optional. Tax audit is undertaken from the tax perspective, and due diligence and other specific audits may be done on a case-to-case basis or as per requirement.

For any kind of audit, an audit trail is important to validate key assertions of any transactions—namely, existence, occurrence, completeness, valuation, obligation, accuracy and presentation. This enables the auditors to verify the authenticity of the transactions. Hence, documentation plays a key role. All transactions undertaken must be sufficiently supported by evidence (such as invoice, proof of payment received for revenue, necessary approvals, purchase order, suppliers invoice, delivery note, vouchers, payment made and so on, for every expense). The auditors will also verify if the transactions are in line with the stated policies and procedures.

Auditors will also look into the internal financial controls, compliance aspects and so on, and the audit opinion in the report is given after a thorough verification of transactions. The auditors normally resort to checking of a sample size of a set transactions, as 100 per cent verification may not be possible. The sample is usually determined based on the materiality levels. The auditors' responsibility is to comment on a true and fair view of the financial statements.

> Reflections:
> - *What are the selection criteria for appointing an auditor for your business?*
> - *List the expectations you have from your auditor in the engagement letter.*
> - *What audit trails are you creating within your business?*

Hiring of Services

> SRI was growing rapidly and the focus was primarily on driving revenue growth. Of the three founders, no one was inclined towards handling the day-to-day nitty-gritties of finance. However, they were keen to know and understand the financial performance of their business. Does this sound familiar to you?

While you may know basic financial concepts and understanding, the routine and mundane aspects of handling finance can be outsourced. The finance function can be performed in-house or outsourced. If it is in-house, the function can be performed by a competent finance person (who may be supervised by you) or an efficient finance team. Your choice between an individual and a team is dependent on the volume of activity/transactions to be handled.

The advantage of outsourcing is that you can focus on the business aspects and develop and strengthen the business further, while the finance experts can handle the matters of finance for you. Further, as rules and regulations keep changing with time, as well as the introduction of new laws and compliances, it is easier if finance functions are outsourced, especially in the initial stages of your business.

On the other hand, the advantage of having the same done in-house is that it is cost effective and provides you with better operational control.

Hiring of services can be evaluated for other lines of operations as well, such as marketing, administration, IT, and so on—depending on the requirement, it may be decided as needed.

Irrespective of whether the services are performed in-house or outsourced, you need to supervise and have good control of these important functions.

> Reflections:
> - *What are the potential areas of your business where you would like to consider outsourcing as an option?*
> - *On what basis would you decide between in-house or outsourcing as the right approach for your business?*
> - *Irrespective of the option you decide on for each area of operation, list the advantages and disadvantages of having services performed in-house versus outsourcing.*

Separation of Funds

> As SRI was a bootstrapped set-up, in many instances, the trio used their personal money to fund many of the business operations. Needless to say, the vice versa was also happening. Once, Sid had paid some of SRI's bills by using his personal credit card. He missed making the credit card payment on time, as he was overwhelmed by the many activities happening in SRI. This resulted in huge interest charges by the bank (to Sid) on the delayed payment.

WHAT THE FINANCE

> Sid felt the interest charges should be borne by SRI, but Isha pointed out that, as the delay was caused by Sid's inefficiency in handling the payment, the amount had to be borne by Sid.

What is your take on the above? Research indicates that one of the reasons businesses fail is the use of business funds for personal use. So, this needs to be avoided. Therefore from a legal standpoint, Isha is correct to state that the delay was caused by Sid, as the onus was on Sid to make the payment.

As a first step, you need to establish a legal framework for your business (as deemed fit). It could be a sole proprietorship, partnership firm, limited liability partnership, private company or others. As your business is a separate legal entity, it is important to segregate the assets, liabilities, revenue and expenses of the entity and the individual.

Obtain a separate bank account for your business. Register for a trademark, goods and services tax (GST) and other appropriate requirements, as applicable. While it can be a challenge, avoid personal guarantees for business loans. An alternative could be to explore financing alternatives that allow your business to borrow money without the requirement of personally guaranteeing the loan.

Keep track of your business' expenditure from the beginning. The right accounting software will assist in keeping your business expenses and personal expenses separate. Take time off periodically to review the transactions of your business, and keep personal transactions segregated from business transactions.

Reflections:

- *What is the method currently in place to segregate your personal and professional transactions?*
- *How will you justify transactions that are grey in nature to the tax authorities?*
- *How will your accounting team know if a particular transaction is personal or professional?*

Tracking of Receipts and Payments

It is important to track all the receivables and payables of your business at periodic intervals (weekly, bi-weekly or monthly, as required), as it ensures follow-up of dues from customers and avoids penalties and interest payments on amounts payable by the business. This will also assist in better cash flow management and business continuity.

> In SRI, the electricity bills were not paid on time, as their accountant was on vacation and no one else thought it was their responsibility to check the dues. This resulted in the service being disconnected. The business loss arising due to this impact was much higher than anticipated, as it resulted in loss of productivity, increased overheads and so on. Hence, it is important that you ensure all transactions happen within the respective timeframe, for which it is essential to track your receipts and payments. This also made the founders realise that it was important to have another person act as a back-up, should the concerned person be away from office.

> Reflections:
>
> - *What is your frequency of tracking receipts and payments?*
> - *How will you know the due dates for receipts and payments?*
> - *Who in your team is responsible for tracking receipts and payments? Who is their back-up?*

Tax Discipline

> SRI's central focus was to improve their internal efficiency. This resulted in them paying little or no attention to other important matters, such as tax discipline. As a start-up, SRI failed to understand the importance of making tax payments on time, and many tax deadlines were missed, which resulted in them paying interest and penalties. Over the years of growth, SRI understood that it was essential to understand the applicable laws in order to avoid paying the interest and penalties.

What is the case with you?

It is best to be on track from the tax perspective in filing the returns within the due dates, remitting the tax amount within the deadlines and being compliant in all aspects of the regulation framework. This includes both income tax, as well as other taxes such as GST. It is a healthy practice to be complaint with tax and other regulatory issues right from the start of operations.

Further, systematic and proper maintenance of the books and records will ensure a smooth and quick closure of the audit or queries that may arise from the income tax department and/or other regulators.

As tax penalties and interest have to be paid in case of non-adherence to the taxes, it is better to be safe and ensure timely payment and file tax returns within the due date.

Note that tax paid is not a tax-deductible expenditure, and any interest or penalty paid is also not allowed as a tax deduction.

> Reflections:
> - *What are the due dates of your applicable compliances?*
> - *How will you be updated on the changes in tax rates, dates and so on?*
> - *Who is the right person to advise you on the business tax matters?*

Keeping the above points as the basics, get started in the right way—right away! As per your business requirements, you can make your own list of the best practices that would be the most suitable for you. The above points were to give you an idea of the various areas where best practices can be implemented. Do take some time to reflect on what other areas of your business you can extend these best practices to. Explore and find out your industry's best practices and fine-tune your list accordingly.

We can now move on to see what you can do to enhance your business performance from the financial perspective.

Chapter 2

WHAT YOU CAN DO

This section will focus on what you can do as the business owner to get your business into good shape from the financial perspective. It is aimed at giving you a better understanding on the aspects you need to pay close attention to.

The topics we will look at in this section are:

- Review of financials
- Forecast
- Variance analysis
- Dashboard
- Business metrics
- Minimum viable product
- Scalable business model
- Selection of banker
- Selection of auditor

Review of Financial Statements

Do you review your financial statements? If yes, how often?

Simply put, review is a study of the financial statements, so that you notice the trends, key ratios, and so on, and come up with ways and means of making the company more effective, and driving the growth and performance of your organisation.

By reviewing the performance of your organisation, you will be able to identify the loopholes and areas that require improvement, and you can focus on them. Alternatively, you could delegate the required action to the concerned team member. It is essential for you to review the financial performance of your organisation on a monthly basis, as it will reveal the financial position and health of your organisation.

This review of financial statements is facilitated by a Management Information System (MIS), which is/are report/s generated by the system. An MIS helps in evaluating business performance and aids in decision-making and tracking of progress.

Some illustrations from SRI can help explain the importance of financial reviews and possible corrective measures.

> **Example 1:**
>
> SRI's sales had been growing over the past 6 months, and the profits reflected in their financial statements were good. However, they noticed that they did not have sufficient funds in the bank. The reason was that their accounts receivable amount was high. After a review of the financial statements, they realised that the collection of dues was not done on time—hence, the bank balance was low and receivables were high. Therefore, the action was to ensure that their receivables were collected immediately.
>
> **Example 2:**
>
> SRI's sales doubled but their margins remained stagnant. This implies that SRI was over-spending. By scrutinising the expense items on a line-by-line basis, they were able to identify the areas where they were spending excessively, and introduce cost-cutting measures.

Example 3:

SRI noticed that, in the current month, there was a big surge in other variable costs. On deeper scrutiny, they realised that it pertained to their grand Annual Day celebrations. After seeing the impact on their P&L, they realised that they had gone overboard and organised a very lavish celebration. They also become aware that they needed to put in more effort to work towards their budgeted profit.

Example 4:

While reviewing their cash flow statements, SRI noticed that a huge chunk had been paid as taxes in that particular month. Upon further investigation, they were informed that, apart from the tax portion, it also included interest and penalty charges accruing from delayed filing. They resolved to never miss filing the returns within the due date, going forward.

Example 5:

After a scrutiny of their financial statements, SRI realised that the amount spent on marketing and advertising for the past one year had not generated sufficient new leads or growth in their business. Hence, the action they decided to take was to downsize the remaining budget by 20 per cent for the remaining year. SRI further decided to utilise the 20 per cent of the remaining budget of the marketing cost in the next financial year as they felt the prospects of getting more clients would be brighter then.

Reflections:

- *Who can help you to understand financial statements better?*
- *What does your financial statement reveal about the financial health of your business?*
- *After reviewing your financial statements, what corrective actions do you think can be taken?*

Forecast

Periodically (say, every quarter), you need to update your budget and prepare a forecast or projected P&L, which will provide a realistic scenario of your business. This is not mandatory but would help you assess your company's performance and serve as a guide on the necessary steps to be taken.

How to prepare your forecast or projections?

Let us say you are at the end of quarter one. Here are the steps you need to take to prepare the projections:

1. Take the actual results of quarter one.
2. Prepare the projected sales and projected expenses for the next 3 quarters.
3. These should be realistic numbers.
4. Add (1.) and (2.) to arrive at the projected numbers for the year-end.
5. Review it and gauge the necessary steps to be taken to meet your desired targets.
6. If you are end of the second quarter, take the actual results for the past 6 months and add the projected numbers for the next 2 quarters and so on.

By undertaking the above exercise, you will know the position you are likely to reach in that year. While preparing forecasts, it is better to adopt a conservative approach, as a pleasant surprise is always more welcome than an unpleasant one.

> To illustrate, let us say SRI has fallen short of the budgeted sales by 25 per cent for quarter one, and the actual expenses are higher than the budgeted expenses by 10 per cent, thereby reducing their budgeted profits at the end of the first quarter. On probing further, Ram figured that the drop in sales was because of lack of communication with his team leaders, who needed to be motivated to achieve their sales targets. Further he felt that the actual expenses were higher than budgeted as the budgets prepared were not realistic. So, he reworked the forecasted expenses to reflect

> the real picture. In order to meet their year-end profit target, they needed to work on improving their revenue; it was also required to take care of the realistic forecasted costs. This gave them a fair picture on the quantum of sales to be achieved over the remaining year to meet their targets. So, SRI found it beneficial to prepare forecasts periodically.

How do you think forecasts will benefit your business?

> **Reflections:**
> - *If you have sales returns after closing the books for the first quarter, what action will you include in your forecasted numbers?*
> - *If you are anticipating a huge order but it is not yet confirmed, what portion of it will you consider in your forecasts?*
> - *How realistic are your forecasted numbers?*

Variance Analysis

> Variance = Budgeted numbers – Actual numbers

While variance refers to the difference between the budget and actuals, variance analysis refers to the quantitative investigation of the difference between the plan and actuals.

Variance analysis is a tool that helps you to evaluate the performance of your business. It helps in cost control as well as cost reduction.

This is an important exercise, as it might reveal to you the lacuna in the system, and further encourage you to dig deeper into the performance and plug the holes. All of this helps propel your business towards better performance.

Variance analysis can be used across all items. For example, the difference between budgeted sales and actual sales is the sales variance. Similarly, variance analysis can be performed on all items, such as material variance, labour variance, overhead variance, stock variance, utilisation variance and so on. Any kind of variance refers to the difference (or variation) from the budgeted numbers and actual numbers.

A positive variance is considered beneficial, as it is favourable, and a negative variance is regarded in the opposite light, as it is unfavourable.

As a business owner, keep a close watch on all your expenses and income on a monthly basis. This will help you to address or correct any deviations in the next month, and help you to recover and get back on track within the same financial year, thereby helping you meet your year-end target. You can also investigate the financial results over multiple periods, with the information listed side-by-side, so that the trends can be observed.

The exercise will also provide you with deeper insights, help you to do a root cause analysis, and aid you in setting things right from the grassroots. Sometimes, it could also help you to plan better and prepare the budget more accurately.

Some illustrations on variance analysis.

> ### Example 1:
>
> While analysing the variance analysis report, SRI noticed a negative variance in the license costs. When they got into the details, it was discovered that they had missed including in the budget the cost of a particular licence, which was essential for one of their software applications. Instances such as these can be avoided if the budget is prepared carefully.
>
> ### Example 2:
>
> There was a significant difference in SRI's recruitment costs in a particular month. They also performed a head-count reconciliation (between the number of new employees recruited with the number of pay outs for recruitment)—and there was no difference. Upon deeper investigation, it was discovered that there was an advance fee paid to a certain recruitment vendor, and this amount was not set off with the subsequent payment, which resulted in this variance.

Example 3:

In a particular month, SRI's sales variance was positive and the profit margin was also higher than usual. However, they had a feeling that it was not true, given that they did not have a robust bank balance. Upon investigation, they discovered that there was duplication of a substantial invoice to a customer, which resulted in inflated profits.

Example 4:

A stock variance report that arose from a surprise stock check revealed a shortage of 10 units of a particular item in stock. Through deeper investigation and with the help of the CCTV cameras, it was found that the culprit who was causing the difference was a staff member.

Example 5:

The project variance report in a particular project showed that the utilisation of the human resources dropped to 60 per cent in a particular month (as against an average of over 80 per cent each month). A probe revealed that the drop in utilisation levels occurred due to multiple reasons, such as leave taken by two of the project members, non-billable activity performed by other project members—which led to a project delay and thereby a cost overrun for the particular project. This project delay was subsequently rectified and made good in the following month.

Reflections:

- *How will you know if the budgets you have allocated are realistic?*
- *How will you plug the major negative variances?*
- *What if some of the variances cannot be fixed in the current period?*

Dashboard

As a business owner, even if you do not have the time or inclination to get into financial details, ensure that you get a complete overview of the business performance by reviewing the dashboard periodically. The dashboard serves as a quick visual comparison of key performance parameters of your business. It also provides a glimpse of all important business data at one go.

The good thing about a dashboard is that you can design and customise it the way you want. It usually reflects the important parameters you want to check with regard to the progress of your entity. For example, your turnover, profit, cash balance, employee headcount and other information that are relevant to your business can be incorporated into the dashboard. You can also include graphs for easy interpretation.

If required, you can have separate dashboards for each department/vertical, or an expense dashboard, sales performance dashboard, asset dashboard or an investment dashboard. You have the choice of including colour schemes to indicate progress, and other colours to serve as warning indicators. For example, green indicates that the progress is on track, red denotes delay or cause of concern, yellow gives a precautionary message and so on.

> Over a period of time, SRI learnt to use the dashboard to their advantage. They learnt this lesson the hard way. At one point in time, the members had not updated themselves on the head count allocation in each project as on a particular date. This resulted in them over committing to newer projects, which resulted in a shortfall of resources towards commencing the projects on time, thereby creating some bitterness with their customers. On hindsight, SRI felt this could have easily been avoided if they had this data at the top of their heads. Some of the other information that SRI reflected in their finance dashboard included current ratio, receivable status, payable status, working capital, industry trends, performance as against the budget, sales in the pipeline, and performance as against the previous year (or quarter or month).

You have the choice of including other indicators that you would like to keep a tab on (such as number of customers, conversion ratio, cost of capital and so on). What else would you choose?

Based on what your dashboard reveals, you can take necessary business actions and make key financial decisions to turn your business in the right direction.

> Reflections:
> - *On what basis will you pick the components that need to be reflected on your dashboard?*
> - *What are the different dashboards you would like to maintain for your business?*
> - *How frequently would you like to review the dashboard?*

Business Metrics

Business metrics are performance indicators of your business. It involves a detailed analysis of your financial results, and displays of measurable values that show the progress of your business. At times, they act as reminders to let you know how far you are from achieving your business goals for that specific period.

As business metrics is also known as Key Performance Indicators (KPI), the dashboard used for representing the metrics is often also called the KPI dashboard.

There are umpteen possible KPIs in any business. You need to track the important ones that will help you to focus on your top business goals.

Here are some indicative KPIs that SRI wanted to track—feel free to modify them as per your requirements:

- Monthly revenue.
- Gross and net margin (preferably vertical wise, if you are dealing with more than one vertical).
- Sales growth (year on year, year to date, quarterly growth, seasonal growth and so on).

- Cost of customer acquisition (i.e., cost of acquiring new customers maybe through marketing, referrals and so on).
- Monthly recurring revenue.
- Number of customers gained and lost.
- Customer retention ratio (ratio of new customers to old).
- Customer satisfaction report (based on feedback from customers).
- Number of leads generated in each month.
- The ratio of lead–to–client conversion.
- The ratio of cross-selling to existing customers (i.e., getting your existing customers to buy your other products or services).
- The traffic in the website.
- Employee satisfaction survey.
- IT and communication cost per employee.
- Connectivity cost per employee.

> Here is an example of how SRI found the business metrics to be a useful indicator: During one such review, the projected IT cost per employee was higher than normal. When SRI looked for details, they were surprised to discover that one of their delivery heads had signed a Purchase Order on behalf of SRI to procure a new software licence. Firstly, this delivery head was not authorised to sign the purchase order on behalf of SRI. However, as he knew the vendors personally, he took the liberty of issuing it on SRI's letterhead. Next, the founders felt that this particular software licence was "good to have" but not a "must have" for SRI. Thus, the Purchase Order was revoked and the company was saved from incurring this cost.

Thus, business metrics will give you good visibility of how your business is progressing. By measuring the right parameters and taking corrective actions, you can steer your business towards better margins.

> **Reflections:**
> - *What are the business metrics you need to focus on?*
> - *With whom does the onus of each business metric lie?*
> - *What was the basis of arriving at the KPIs?*

Minimum Viable Product

If you are in the product space, one of the initial steps you need to take as an entrepreneur is to come up with your minimum viable product (MVP). In other words, your product should have just enough features to get the buy-in from your early customers, obtain feedback and improvise your product thereafter. As a result, you will seek, measure and build on feedback, which will enable a better and higher version of your product.

In order to get to the MVP, you must first have the proof of concept (POC) ready. Once the POC is established, the next step is to set up the prototype. A prototype is a means of testing the feasibility of your POC. The prototype is usually designed for the stakeholders or a minimum audience to showcase your product. The prototype is not for sale. Once the prototype is up and running, the next is the MVP, which is basic and functional in nature and is meant for sale to initial customers. Your final product is usually an improvised version of your MVP.

> SRI had designed their MVP at the starting point of their business. They received valuable inputs from their mentors, professors and some industry experts. This led to SRI understanding the pain points and perspectives of their customers, as well as feedback from the experts, thus resulting in an improved final product.

Some of the advantages that SRI enjoyed through designing their MVP were:

- Lower cost of implementation
- Quick release into the market
- Avoiding failures and capital losses
- Earning while learning

- Providing scope for improvement
- Getting direct feedback from customers
- Catering to the needs of customers in a better way

> **Reflections:**
> - *What will you do if the POC is a failure model?*
> - *How can you improvise the POC to be a great MVP?*
> - *What do you think is the right price for your MVP? How will you substantiate it?*

Scalable Business Model

A scalable business model is one wherein there is a possibility to move your current business to the next level, whereby the revenue grows and leads to increased profits. In other words, when the current business has the potential to cope, perform and grow, it is said to be a scalable business model.

The scalability of your business model can be either horizontal or vertical. Horizontal scalability is the ability to increase capacity by connecting multiple entities, so that they can work as a single unit. Vertical scalability, on the other hand, is the ability to increase the capacity by adding resources. Either way, when a business is scalable, it helps the business to grow both in terms of revenue and profits. Therefore, it is good to have a business model that is open-ended and seeks to improve and grow continuously.

> SRI realised that having a scalable business model was a key criterion that investors look for, as it promises a growth-oriented organisation that is forward looking. For scaling, SRI had to take into account the extra investment required, other resources required (including human resources) and plan accordingly. Preparing a plan of scalability gave a clear road map ahead—not only for them but also to their potential investors. While evaluating the scalable options, apart from introducing newer verticals, they also

> examined the possibilities of extending across geographies, which helped them to work on the areas that they needed to improve, in order to penetrate to the newer markets. Remember, scalability is one of the key parameters that investors look for.

Is your business scalable?

However you need to be cautious as to not to rush up the scalability too quickly, as in the case of housing.com—which headed for a fiasco. As per the words of founder Rahul Yadav (who was sacked from the start-up he created, after 3 years), "We scaled up too fast. We should have actually cracked one market completely before venturing out into any other market. If I were to look at Housing.com again, I would rather crack the model locally and keep refining it before taking it anywhere else in the country. I would scale up for profitability than for burning."

> **Reflections:**
> - *What are your thoughts on scaling your business?*
> - *How will you know if your business model is scalable?*
> - *How will you cope with the growth of your business on account of scaling up?*

Selection of Auditor

Auditors and financial consultants play a significant role in partnering with you in your financial growth and success. Hence, it is essential to choose the people for these roles with care and caution. Some pointers that SRI used are given here, as they may aid you in your decision. If you have an existing auditor, you can evaluate him/her against some of the following parameters.

- Your auditor can also be your financial advisor but not vice-versa.
- For either of the roles, it is better to select a firm that provides the required services.

- Check on the level of experience and knowledge they carry with themselves.
- Seek their existing client testimonials.
- Check if their principles and values match with yours.
- Find out how they can contribute to your financial growth and success.
- Evaluate how well they understand your business operations.
- Assess how well can they contribute to your tax planning.
- Will they be a good fit in the long-term and be able to handhold your organisation in times of need?
- You may want to look for the level of trust, comfort, working rapport and their mastery over the subject.
- Meet a few more people before finalising so that it can help you evaluate based on some of the above-mentioned parameters.
- Explicitly state your requirements to avoid ambiguity.
- Negotiate before agreeing on the pricing offered to you for their services.

Some of the above pointers can also be used to select your legal consultant, IT consultant and so on.

Reflections:
- *Prepare a list of expectations you have from your auditor/financial consultant.*
- *How will you know if your auditor/consultant is proactive?*
- *In your opinion, with whom does the onus of managing finances lie?*

Selection of Banker

A majority of your business transactions are done through the bank—therefore, it is important to establish a good relationship with the right bank, which can cater to your requirements. Here are some pointers used by SRI, which you may refer to for selecting the right kind of bank for your business. If you have an existing preferred bank, you can evaluate it against some of the following parameters.

- Credibility of the bank.
- Level of security for your funds.
- Structure of the bank's charges that you are likely to incur.
- Facilities they are offering to your business.
- Will they meet your long-term requirements?
- Proximity of the branch to your place of work.
- Online facilities offered.
- How will you rate the ease of obtaining credit facility for your operational requirements?
- Interest rates that are being offered on fixed deposits and interest charges on your borrowing/credit card utilisation.
- What is the minimum balance that you are required to have with the bank?
- What are the customer services that are being offered to you?
- Option of having your employees' salary accounts in the same bank.
- Check with your other contacts who use the bank, and get their opinions on the latter's efficiency and service.
- The rates the bank is extending for sweep facility, foreign exchange rates, ATM charges and so on.
- How well does the shortlisted bank cater to all your requirements?
- If you are dealing in foreign exchange, how good is their treasury team?
- Compare your choice with a few other banks that are offering the required services you need.
- For practical purposes, it is sufficient to use one bank that can cater to all your needs. However, if you want to get the most competitive rates, it may be a good idea to engage with at least 2 banks, so as to get the best rates/deals for most of your banking transactions.

> **Reflections:**
> - *What are your criteria for selecting your banker?*
> - *What are the top priorities you want from your banker?*
> - *What do you think about having multiple bank accounts for your business?*

This brings us to the end of this section. In the next section, we are going to see what will keep the bread and butter of your business going. We will look into aspects that will help your revenue to grow, thereby increasing your top line and resulting in increased bottom line. I will also provide some suggestions and reflections, which can contribute towards your overall revenue growth, for you to keep in mind.

Chapter 3

WHAT WILL KEEP YOU GOING

Irrespective of which business you are in, you need to have regular revenue stream that will help you to grow and sustain your business. When your revenue grows, there is a high probability that your profits will also grow.

This section touches on the ways and means by which you can keep your revenue ticking. It will address matters such as how to arrive at the right pricing, sources to get other forms of revenue, loopholes that can be avoided, and some care and caution that can be taken so as to maximise your revenue earning potential.

Let us look into some of the common challenges in this area and how you can overcome them.

Perceived Value

> SRI was not sure about how to develop their pricing strategy. They were concerned that if they overpriced, they would fail to attract many customers and also succumb to competition. If they underpriced, they would lose out on profits. They were struggling to determine the right value of their offerings and further wanted to understand the impact of perceived value on pricing. They also debated amongst themselves on a good time to offer pricing discounts or to increase their prices. Are you facing a similar dilemma?

Perceived value can act as a good pricing strategy. As the name suggests, perceived value is the worth a customer associates with your product or service. Normally, customers are unaware of the factors involved in pricing as well as the estimated costs of production or cost of sales. What customers rely on are factors such as utilisation value, emotional appeal, your competitors' offerings, aesthetic sense and so on, as well as their belief in the benefit they will derive from your product or service.

Therefore, perceived value actually translates into the value your customer is willing to pay for your goods, product or service. Customers arrive at the value, based on the product or service's ability to fulfil a need, provide a solution or afford satisfaction. Thus, your marketing team can work on enhancing the perceived value of your product or service and eventually arrive at the pricing of your product, through which you can ensure easier saleability.

Remember, individual perceptions vary. If the customers can obtain utility from what you have to offer, or if they are able to seek benefits that are not available from any other sources, the perceived utility value is high.

So, SRI understood that, to arrive at a better pricing strategy, they should focus on how to work on the perceived value of their product or service. They also strategised on periodic discounts (during festive times) and looked at increasing their prices only after a year.

Suggestions:
- Evaluate the ways and means of enhancing the perceived value of your offering.
- Step into the customer's shoes to see what could be the perceived value.
- The value that you are offering your customer could be form utility, task utility, time utility, place utility or possession utility.
- The brand also plays a role on arriving at the perceived value—what is your brand value/brand reputation?
- Remember that the perceived value of luxury goods is high, as it enhances the joy quotient, status and prestige of the users.

> **Reflections:**
> - *What can you do differently, when compared to your competitors?*
> - *What is it about your product (or service) that will create an impact (or appeal) to your customer?*
> - *What is the advantage the customer gains by using your product or service?*

Pricing

> SRI did not know how to arrive at the right pricing for their offerings—an issue that is commonly faced by many entrepreneurs. They initially arrived at the price on an ad-hoc basis, only to realise that they were not covering all their costs. And when they increased the prices, they did not get sufficient customers. SRI was wondering what they ought to do to set it right. Do you face the same issue, too?

Arriving at the right pricing for your product or service can be a challenging task. While over-pricing could lead to loss of customers/potential customers, lower pricing could result in losses/lower margins. Hence, it is essential to arrive at the right pricing strategy.

There are many factors that play a role in the pricing strategy for your product/service. These could include both internal and external factors. Internal factors could be the costs incurred, working capital requirement, utilisation level and so on, while the external factors could be the industry trends, tax on raw materials, foreign exchange fluctuation, interest rates, government policy and so on.

While internal factors are usually within the ambit of your control, you may not have much say about the external factors. So, from your side, much attention and focus needs to be provided on minimising the costs, maximising the efficiencies, keeping adequate levels of margins, providing for a buffer (for the external factors), and then arriving at the best possible price for the relevant product/service.

Prices will vary for each product/service, depending on the market demand, level of quality, supply chain, the unique selling point, the special features it offers and so on.

Further, remember that under-pricing need not necessarily be welcomed by your target customers. For example, Nano cars did not take off as well as expected due to the 'cheap in price' image it had created for itself.

SRI used the above, and the suggestions given below, to arrive at their ideal pricing.

Suggestions:

- Compute the total costs you are incurring to manufacture your product or render service.
- Arrive at the desired level of margin required.
- Note that the sum of the costs and the margin can help you arrive at the pricing. For example, if the sum of all your costs is 80 and the margin required is 20, the price arrived at could be 100.
- You will have to check if your pricing strategy is in line with the industry standards. Unless there is something extra or unique about your product or service, the pricing is to be in line with the industry standard.
- In an ideal scenario, one-third of the selling price should be the total of your costs, another one-third should go towards the margin and the remaining one-third should contribute to the reserves. You have to check the feasibility of this, depending on your industry.
- Study the industry trends and become aware of the prices the competitors are offering for similar products/services.
- Check if the margin and pricing are in line with the market standards.
- If the initial costs of product development are high, the pricing strategy should aim to recover these costs over a set period of the product life cycle.
- If your prices are higher than your competitors', find out ways and means of optimising costs, thereby decreasing prices and maintaining reasonable margins.
- If your prices are lower, you may want to look at increasing your margins—if it is not in line with the industry, unless you have made a conscious choice to attract customers.

- Alternatively, if your prices are lower and margins are reasonable, look at ways of increasing your market share.
- Remember to include in the price other auxiliary services you may be offering (such as free after sales service, warranty period and so on).
- Identify emerging trends.

> **Reflections:**
> - *If you were the customer, what amount would you pay for your company's offerings?*
> - *What is the value quotient you are offering?*
> - *Evaluate perceived threats by hypothetically pricing your product or service at a higher level/lower level.*

Revenue Recognition

SRI was informed by their auditors about the concept of revenue recognition. SRI was intrigued that this could influence their bottom line. Do you know what it meant?

As an entrepreneur, you need to be aware of the concept of revenue recognition as it can impact your P&L. I have noticed many instances wherein there is a huge difference between the pre-audited and post-audited numbers. Revenue recognition could be one such reason. This one item can sometimes convert your huge profit into loss at one go. So, what is revenue recognition? And how does it impact profit? I will explain the concept through a simple example.

> SRI has bagged a contract for Rs. 60 lakhs for one year from a customer. The contract period was for the calendar year, January to December. SRI has received the entire amount as advance on 30 December—2 days before the commencement of the contract. SRI's financial year-end for book closure was 31 March. What was the amount of revenue that is to be recognised for the year ending 31 March?

> If SRI planned to recognise the entire amount of Rs. 60 lakhs as revenue for the year ended 31 March, it is incorrect—the reason being it pertained to the 12-month period from January to December. The amount to be recognised as revenue for the period from January to March had to be pro-rated for 3 months (assuming the work was as per schedule, as on 31 March). So, the revenue to be entered in SRI's books on 31 March was Rs. 15 lakhs. The remaining Rs. 45 lakhs was to be recognised as revenue for the next financial year, as it pertained to that financial period.
>
> Now let us tweak the above example a bit. SRI's customer had not paid any advance amount in December. Instead, he paid the entire amount of Rs. 60 lakhs on 30 June. Now, what is the amount that is to be recognised as revenue?
>
> There is no change on the amount to be recognised, as Rs. 15 lakhs pertains to the first financial year, and the remaining for the next financial year.
>
> Importantly, note that revenue recognition is independent of the receipt of cash.
>
> SRI felt relieved on understanding revenue recognition, as they felt they were better prepared to answer the queries of their board of directors and not be embarrassed with fluctuating margins pre- and post-audit.

This is a very important distinction as this concept can turn around your entire financial statements. There is also a case of distinction between cash profit and the actual profit. In the example, with the advance amount received, your cash balance increases but your actual profit will be different.

Revenue recognition is a generally accepted accounting principle. It is an accounting principle wherein revenue is recognised as per specific conditions or events.

Suggestions:

- As this is an accounting principle, there is nothing much to suggest. However, if there is going to be a significant impact on your profits, consult your financial advisor beforehand.

- Remember, based on the revenue recognition principle, the related costs also need to be apportioned to the respective financial years.
- Depending on the types of services that are being offered (such as warranty, free service and so on), the proportionate revenue and costs will be deferred at the time of incurring the same.

> Reflections:
> - *What are the current contracts that run into different financial years?*
> - *Are the current contracts in line with the schedule of delivery? If not, what is the impact on the revenue?*
> - *Compute the total anticipated costs for the respective contracts that require to be spread across the financial years.*

Utilisation

> SRI had many resources in the form of employees, assets, office space and so on. SRI was wondering how to ensure maximum utilisation of these available resources. One of the areas they wanted to explore as a standard practice was on knowledge transfer. SRI also wanted to allocate a suitable timeframe for knowledge transfer when a person quit their organisation or moved to another project. They wondered what could be the right time period to be allocated for knowledge transfer between their resources. Do you face a similar concern?

Each business thrives on the resources it has. A business has various resources that work on the day-to-day operations—they can be in terms of the people or assets that contribute towards the daily operations. From a financial perspective, a tab is to be kept on the efficiency levels of the contribution of the resources as the efficiency levels or the output of the resources is directly proportional to the revenue stream of the business (this is under the assumption that there is constant demand for the product or services offered).

WHAT THE FINANCE

As the business owner, you have to ensure that the resources are working effectively and that their efforts translate into your revenue.

Suggestions:

- Have some measures in place to check the efficiency levels and contribution of each resource.
- Find out their current efficiency levels of operation.
- The resource efficiency can be measured in terms of the output in relation to the number of hours spent/billability or maybe in terms of products manufactured/delivered.
- A method to be arrived at to keep idle time at bay.
- Allot a reasonable time period for knowledge transfer (say a week or two depending on the size of the project).
- Should there be any idle resources, options can be evaluated on whether the resources can be productively deployed in other projects.
- Are there any possibilities of outsourcing the extra resources to enhance revenue?
- Explore possibilities of group synergy too, with similar operators/service providers.

Reflections:

- *How do you think you can enhance your business efficiency levels?*
- *What does your utilisation rate indicate?*
- *What are the other ways to improve the utilisation rate?*

Confirmed Orders

> SRI had instances when they had manufactured products (sometimes even customised them specifically) in anticipation of an order from an existing customer (or a prospective customer), but suffered a huge loss when the order never went through.

> Another time, SRI had recruited employees upfront in lieu of an upcoming project, but the project never went through, leaving SRI with the burden of excess costs and no revenue.
>
> Due to such past, bitter, experiences, SRI wanted to find out how to identify a confirmed order for their products and services. They did not want to burn their fingers again, and wanted to know how to prevent incurring unsold goods/services. Have you had such instances where, after customising the product or deploying resources to work on the project as per your customer requirements, your customer rejected them?

Why do such cases happen? How can you avoid falling into such traps?

In SRI's case, the customer had expressed the intention of placing the order but had not actioned it. Expressing an intention is based on verbal confirmation—however, that does not construe for real due to lack of 'proof' in the legal world.

If you were in such a situation, what should you do?

Unless a written/confirmed Purchase Order is received, do not assume the order is yours. You may want to take chances at times for the fear of not wanting to lose prospective business. It is alright so long as you are cognisant of the fact, and prepared with alternatives should you not receive the order for whatever reasons—more so, if you can manage successfully with such consequences.

I have seen cases wherein the customer's intention was genuine while placing the order. However, the customer failed to get internal approvals, had a change in business plans internally, found a better alternative, or the respective person was no longer associated with the customers' organisation. And as a result, the business had to suffer the impact and pay the price for it.

Suggestions:

- Do not rely on verbal confirmation alone.
- Ensure that you receive a confirmed Purchase Order from your customer with clearly stated terms and conditions.

- It is even better if you can obtain a 50 per cent advance—if not, at least a token amount as advance—from the customer.
- Remember that even with a confirmed Purchase Order, a customer can cancel it (subject to the terms mentioned in the Purchase Order).
- It is better not to undertake manufacturing of customer-specific products without obtaining a substantial amount as advance.
- A similar principle applies for recruitment of employees for new projects. In case of an emergency during project delivery, it is best that you hire temporary staff either for a fixed duration or fixed delivery, and let go of those staff thereafter—if there are no other suitable opportunities for such staff within your organisation.
- Apply prudent business judgement in anticipating orders and follow it up with a written Purchase Order and advance.

> Reflections:
> - *What is your internal policy with regard to obtaining confirmed customer orders?*
> - *What will happen if a much-expected order does not come along?*
> - *How can you be prepared should a large order seeking immediate/quick delivery come your way?*

Marketing And Revenue

> SRI was wondering about the right time when they could market their offerings. They felt that, during the festive times, their sales had a good potential to increase. However, during the other months, the sales were a bit lull. So, SRI felt that they needed to invest in marketing during the quiet times in order to ensure it contributed to increasing their sales. Do you think there is a right time period to sell your business offerings? What do you think is the right time to market your offerings?

While marketing should be ongoing, as it helps boost your income, it is vital to plan the marketing initiatives at the right times to enjoy the most benefits. Timing of marketing initiatives plays a crucial part. The timing is linked to the season, industry trends, your competitors and other economic factors (such as demonetisation) and so on.

Sometimes the timing can be related to just your own internal set-up. For instance, SRI incurred huge marketing costs on promoting some of their new products. Just as the orders started pouring in, they realised that their factory was not sufficiently equipped to handle the quantum of new orders. Thus, it was not only marketing costs gone down the drain, but also loss of revenue and bad reputation in the market.

Hence, strategic planning is essential. Marketing initiatives undertaken during lean periods may be a good idea. It might also be a good bet to undertake marketing efforts to offset your competitor's campaign.

Before launching new products, you may want to undertake a market survey, study the new markets, customers, geographies and so on, and do a complete market research study to ensure you are competing in the right market and at the right time.

It is good to incur marketing spending at the right time to boost your top line and thereby increase your margins. Utilise the spending effectively.

Suggestions:

- Keep in mind that the timing of marketing is crucial.
- Be ready to handle higher volumes that result from the marketing drive.
- Have you thought of innovative ways of using digital marketing/social media marketing to reach out to potential and new customers?
- You may also want to resort to guerrilla marketing techniques to boost your revenue, especially in the initial stages where you may not have the luxury of investing much money into marketing.
- Does the season influence your customer's buying patterns (for instance, air-conditioners' sale tends to increase during the summer months)?
- Identify marketing experts who are versatile/proficient with regard to your industry.

> **Reflections:**
> - *Identify the right target audience to utilise your marketing spend effectively.*
> - *What are the best avenues to market your product/service?*
> - *How equipped are you to deliver higher customer volumes?*

Charges to The Client

> One of SRI's clients wanted 5 resources from SRI to work out of their premises for a period of 6 months. SRI agreed to their request. They did not negotiate for any extra charges as they did not think about the additional transportation and other associated costs. So, in effect, SRI was incurring charges on behalf of their client, especially as the client's location was far away from SRI's office. This resulted in increased expenses. Have you also faced a similar situation?

Similarly, sometimes, you may incur expenses that are incurred exclusively on behalf of your customer. It could be a certain type of tax, or charges such as stationery charges, transportation charges, travel costs or other costs that can be directly attributable to a specific project or customer. Such expenses are sometimes referred to as 'out of pocket expenses'.

The fees you have quoted to your customer is likely to be only for the product or service agreed upon, and these extra charges will directly eat away into your profits if you are incurring these amounts on behalf of your client. During my interaction with one start-up founder, I discovered that he was not aware that a specific tax, which could actually be recharged to his clients, was being incurred as part of his business. This was eating away directly into his profits.

So, what can you do about such amounts that hit your margins? It is in your own interest that you do not bear the brunt of such expenses. Hence, it is best to pass on such costs back to your customer.

Suggestions:

- Ensure that the PO received from your customer clearly states the value as 'excluding applicable taxes'/'other applicable charges'.
- The agreement/SOW with your client should have a provision of recharging the out of pocket expenses back to the customer.
- Be watchful of direct and specific customer-related costs, and remember to charge them back to the respective customer.
- Remember to include these amounts in your invoice. You can set it up in your accounting software at the time of accounting, so that you do not have to track the recharging of each and every item.
- Invoice these charges to your client and collect them immediately as they impacts your cash flow.

Reflections:

- *What is your policy for charging out of pocket expenses?*
- *Who is monitoring/keeping tab of such rechargeable expenses?*
- *What is your recovery period for such expenses?*

Notice Period

SRI's current year's budgeted turnover was based on certain assumptions. As per their estimate, a particular client would have contributed over 40 per cent of their turnover. However, due to unforeseen circumstances, the customer terminated the contract with immediate effect—which resulted in an unforeseen crisis, and caused them to panic. To make things worse, the overall revenue budget that was prepared was, in fact, not a realistic one, thus affecting their entire performance for the year. So, with a big customer gone and incorrect budgets, SRI was in hot soup. Sounds familiar to you?

The customer's termination not only affected SRI's turnover but also increased their associated costs with regard to that order. How can you stay clear of such scenarios?

> To make it worse, another customer of SRI, who was in a financial mess, delayed payments and kept making false promises of settling the dues. This affected SRI cash flow and, in turn, they were unable to pay their suppliers and vendors on time. How would you tackle such issues?

The easiest way to avoid such issues is by clearly stating the notice period for termination, as well as the notice period for settling dues.

Suggestions:

- At the time of entering into a contract/agreement with your customers, ensure that you insert 2 clauses pertaining to the above challenges.
    - One is in the termination clause in the agreement, which has to clearly state that the contract can be terminated only after the notice period of a certain number of days (for example, 30 or 60 days, or as per the case).
    - In order to get your dues on time, you can insert an interest clause on delayed payments, if the dues go beyond an unacceptable period of time. In reality, you may not want to enforce the interest clause. However, it is good to have it in the agreement as a safety precaution, should the matter go beyond your control in recovering the dues from certain customers. Also, note that all clients may not agree to have the interest clause on delayed payments. Use your discretion and decide accordingly.
- By including such clauses, you are safeguarding your interests and, at the same time, also having a leeway with the client, should the situation warrant that you have to resort to legal recourse.

> **Reflections:**
> - *What is your Plan B if a customer were to cancel his/her order?*
> - *What would be the most favourable terms and conditions (for you) in the notice period for your customers?*
> - *What steps can you put in place to secure timely collection of dues?*

Prevention of Revenue Leakage

Revenue leakage is simply the result of lost billing opportunities. It arises when a client has not been billed for the service your organisation has rendered or not billed a product that has been delivered. This happens because the organisation missed raising an invoice to the customer, thereby giving away products or services for free.

> In the case of SRI, the person responsible for invoicing had met with an accident and was on long leave. No one else was entrusted with the responsibility, as no one else knew how to go about it, and nor did anyone think it was important to raise an invoice on time. One customer wanted to raise the invoice for payment. After following up specifically with Isha, it was sent. However, the other invoices were left unattended.
>
> It was during the audit that SRI's auditors pointed out cases of revenue leakage, which was a cause of worry for the trio. As per their auditor's advice, they wanted to ensure that:
>
> - That they raised an invoice on time to the client for services rendered/product delivered.
> - That clients were billed for all the work performed/supplies delivered.
> - That they plugged leaks of any sort in the revenue system.

Has this happened to you? How can you take precautionary steps to prevent them?

You have to be conscious about preventing revenue leakages, which leads to eating away into profits right away. Checks and balances have to be put in place to prevent revenue leaks.

This may not pose as big a challenge during the initial stages, as the organisation is still in its nascent stage and revenues may be at a minimum, thus making it easier to ensure that nothing is amiss. However, it might sometimes become difficult to keep track of whether all the assignments/consignments undertaken have been billed to the respective client or not.

If you missed raising an invoice, remember that your customer cannot pay you without you demanding for it (i.e., through an invoice). This impacts both your top line and bottom line, and affects your cash flow as well. Hence, sufficient precautionary steps must be taken to ensure timely and consistent billing.

In SRI's case, reasons for revenue leaks were due to a variety of reasons, such as lack of clarity within the business, lack of automation, lacuna in the revenue system, lack of communication between the teams and so on, which they managed to set right.

In my corporate career, I have seen instances where some small- or medium-sized vendor organisations missed out on raising invoices for either services rendered or products delivered, thus losing out on valuable opportunities.

It is also essential that the invoices be raised on time. There may be instances where you may have realised that an invoice was not raised (say, after a year). By then, there are chances that the client has also forgotten, or there is a change in management. Also, the client may simply refuse to pay after a long delay as the books for the previous year have been closed. Whatever the case, your chances or recovering the amount later becomes slim. Hence, it is in your best interest to raise invoices within the stipulated time.

Suggestions:

- It would be a healthy practice to start by reviewing all your billings for each month.
- Compare revenues on a month-on-month basis and reconcile it with the orders received/lost. Is it in line with reality? If not, look for logical reasons.
- If you are a manufacturing organisation, link invoicing with stock movement. As soon as stock is sent out, an invoice should be generated. It would be ideal if the process were automated.
- If you are a service-based organisation, an effective and efficient time-tracking system needs to be enforced, whereby the effort spent on a customer is tracked and billed. It would also be a good

practice to reconcile all billable employees against project-wise billings to avoid leaks.
- Are efficient internal controls in place to prevent revenue leaks?
- Are your employees trained to ensure that their respective clients are billed? If not, they must be able to raise a reminder in the system to complete billing. There must be clear communication between the sales team, service team and support staff.
- If there are contracts/annual maintenance contracts that are to be renewed, there needs to be a specific process in place to track these.
- New revenue opportunities that are lost translate to revenue leaks. Are there steps in place to prevent these?
- An invoice is to be raised periodically in line with the service level agreements (SLAs).
- Finally, if you aware that a particular customer has not been billed on the due date, raise an invoice immediately and track your dues.

> Reflections:
> - *What is the process you have in place to ensure that no revenue leaks occur?*
> - *How have you customised your accounting software to handle revenue leaks?*
> - *Apart from you, who is keeping tab of the revenue process?*

Marginal Revenues

SRI was advised by their consultants to focus on marginal revenues to maximise their revenues. While they wanted to maximise their income, there were not sure what exactly marginal revenue meant. Do you know what it means?

Increasing revenue is what all entrepreneurs wish for—just like you. Ideally, revenues can be increased by increasing the number of customers, increasing the selling price, increasing the quantum of sales with existing customers (by wooing them with volume discounts, for example), or by increasing the average transaction size.

Apart from these factors, it would be ideal for you to think about increasing marginal revenues.

Marginal revenue is the additional revenue that will be generated by the sale of one extra unit. It arises from the unit revenue of the last item sold. This lowers the price of all units sold. Marginal revenue can remain constant over a certain level of output. However, with increased quantum, the marginal revenue could decrease.

> For example, in SRI, if the sale from 10 units were to generate a revenue of Rs. 1,000 and the sale from the eleventh unit were to generate Rs. 90, the marginal revenue of the eleventh unit is Rs. 90. It disregards the previous average of Rs. 100 per unit, as it considers only the incremental change. This calculation, along with the calculation of the marginal costs, provided SRI with the flexibility to price their product according to seasonal fluctuations and market demand.

Similarly, marginal cost is the total cost of selling one extra unit. Marginal costs help in controlling costs better and aids in better decision-making. The difference between the marginal revenue and marginal costs is the marginal profit. When marginal revenue is greater than marginal cost, it implies further profits for the company. If the marginal cost is higher, it implies a loss and that it is no longer profitable to sell.

What are your marginal revenues and marginal costs?

Suggestions:

- Evaluate ways and means of optimising revenues by looking at various options such as exploring new territories, allied products, cross-selling and so on.
- Think of unique ways of marketing your product with no or minimal expenses (you can refer to *Guerrilla Marketing* by Pravin Shekhar for some ideas).
- Think out of the box with innovative initiatives.
- Further, step into the shoes of your customer/potential customer to see a different perspective.

- Lastly, define what makes your product or service unique and strategise on your unique selling points.

> **Reflections:**
> - *What are the factors influencing your marginal revenue and marginal costs?*
> - *In what ways can you minimise your marginal costs?*
> - *How can you increase marginal revenue?*

Sweep Facility

> At a networking event, Ram was asked how SRI manages with the extra funds they had. Ram said they park it in their bank account as their fund requirements could vary depending on their receipts and payments. However, when Ram heard about sweep facility to maximise other earnings, he was surprised as neither he nor his co-founders were aware of such a facility. Ram was told that such a facility was offered by banks. Now that he had a clue, he asked SRI's bankers about it. Do you know what it is and how it could help your business?

A sweep account is a bank account that automatically transfers amounts that exceed or fall short of a certain level into a higher interest-earning investment option at the close of each business day. Auto sweep is a facility that interlinks the savings bank account with a fixed deposit account, wherein the amount in excess of a certain limit is automatically transferred to a fixed deposit account that fetches a higher interest.

Since this is an automatic feature, once set up, human intervention is minimal. SRI opted for this facility in order to maximise their interest earnings, which contributed to enhancing their profits.

Suggestions:
- First, assess if you have periodic excess funds that are not fully utilised. Compute the quantum of the amount available. The past

trend of the funds utilised and future cash projections will assist in computing this amount.
- Talk to your banker and ask if this facility is offered to your business.
- If yes, negotiate on the best terms and conditions.
- Set up the limits for the auto sweep.
- Do a random check of the interest computation based on the amount that has been credited to your account.
- Review this facility periodically and make changes as necessary over a period of time.
- Note that the bank usually deducts tax at source on the interest payments.

> **Reflections:**
> - *What are the other options you have, to best utilise the extra cash that you have?*
> - *Any other ways to generate revenue from the excess funds?*
> - *Compute the duration when you would require the funds to be utilised.*

Liquid Funds

> Just when SRI felt that sweep facility was a great way to generate some extra funds, they got know about liquid funds. SRI was told that, in order to gain the maximum from idle funds, investing in liquid funds was a good option. Wanting to know more about it, they engaged in a conversation with their financial consultant about this. Are you also intrigued by this term?
>
> SRI had times when bouts of capital pumped in as their business grew. However, not all of the amounts were to be utilised immediately, as it was subject to the business requirement and business growth. Similarly, there were instances when their customer had paid huge advances and SRI knew that the majority of the cash would remain idle for the next 2 months. These excess

> funds were idle funds, and they had the potential to grow in value. SRI invested the excess funds into liquid funds as advised by their consultant, and SRI was extremely glad to earn the extra revenue from this option.

Whenever there are such excess funds, in all probability, the entire amount is not likely to get consumed immediately. In such a scenario, it is best to deploy the excess funds into liquid funds, liquid-plus funds or ultra-short-term funds or similar such funds.

Liquid fund is a debt mutual fund that invests your money into very short-term market instruments with minimal risk (as compared to other mutual funds). The maturity period is up to 91 days. They can be invested for a minimum of 7 days onwards. The rate of interest offered is higher than bank interest rates. Liquid-plus funds are also similar to liquid funds with a higher average maturity period compared to liquid fund. The funds are normally invested into commercial papers, treasury bills, term deposits etc. These funds have no lock-in period and are open-ended schemes. Redemption happens within a day. Liquid funds are considered the least risky.

This method can also be opted when there are huge amounts of money that have been paid by a customer, and you do not foresee any significant cash outflow for the next few weeks or months, thereby gaining extra interest income.

Suggestions:

- Liquid funds act as ideal parking grounds for the excess funds available.
- If interested in pursuing or exploring any of these short-term investment options, consult with expert wealth advisors, who can help you with the right choice based on your requirements, which will help you to maximise the returns.
- A word of caution: Chose the right wealth advisor—one who is well experienced to handle your monies, as the level of risk in these funds could vary.

- Remember to negotiate on the charges of the wealth advisor. Some of them do not charge if the volumes are high as they may get commissions from the funds.
- Understand the tax impact of this interest income on the business. The wealth consultant/financial advisor can help you with it.

> **Reflections:**
> - *Who can help you to arrive at the best option in computing the amount to be invested in liquid funds?*
> - *Any other investments that can generate better or equal returns?*
> - *How frequently do you assess the situation to check on the availability of your excess funds?*

I trust the above would have given you some ideas on how else you can grow your top line. You can also assess other ethical ways by which you can maximise your revenue and grow your profits. Remember that growing your revenue helps in the overall growth of your company. As revenue grows, you need to be watchful of the internal processes that are in place, as it needs to match the size of your business volumes.

Apart from these, the other important aspects you need to be careful of are your expenses and cash outflow. It does not make business sense if all the revenue you earn were eaten away by your expenses. So, let us now analyse costs to see what are the best ways to optimise them and gain better margins for your business.

Chapter 4

WHAT IS YOUR SPEND

We have already seen the difference between cost control and cost reduction. (Refer to Page 24).

Based on your requirements and the internal culture of your organisation, the areas of cost control and cost reduction may be looked into. Sometimes, the term 'cost reduction' may not be welcomed by your team. However, if you can look at ways and means to optimise your costs, it could help in achieving a win-win situation between the teams and the margins.

What is Cost Optimisation?

Cost optimisation is an alternate way of finding the most cost-effective method within the given constraints. It focuses on the business while driving cost reduction, yet maximising the value for the business. Thus, it helps in achieving high performance by maximising the desired factors (such as better pricing, better terms and conditions, and so on) and minimising the undesired factors (such as penalty clause, undue delay and so on) without compromising on the outcome.

One of the ways of evaluating a particular spend is by estimating the value it creates to the system.

Both cost reduction and cost optimisation fuel growth—they are important ingredients for an organisation's long lasting financial success.

Kinds of Costs

The costs that you incur can be classified into many different types of costs—for example, fixed costs (such as rent, which are not proportional to your revenue), variable costs (costs that vary with your revenue) as well as direct and indirect costs, marginal costs and so on. For a better understanding, I am also providing you an overview of the different kinds of costs that a business could have. By analysing the costs and breaking them down further, you can optimise the cost efficiency better.

Sunk Costs

A sunk cost (also known as stranded cost) is a cost that has already been incurred, and which cannot be recovered. These costs cannot be refunded or reduced. Sunk costs should not be considered while making future decisions, as these costs are unrecoverable. For example, previously spent amounts on advertising, research and development and so on, have no bearing on current decisions that will affect the future. The costs of the past should not be a reason to continue spending—the decision should be based on current market conditions.

Opportunity Costs

This is a notional cost, as this cost is not incurred in reality. It is the cost of a perceived benefit over another. It can also be viewed as an alternative that is given up when a decision is made. For example, the amount spent on obtaining some equipment (decision between buying or leasing of an equipment) is an example. Taking opportunity cost into account helps in making the best economic decision for an organisation.

Differential Cost

As the name signifies, the difference in cost between two alternative decisions is known as differential cost. This is used to differentiate between the multiple options to choose the ideal one. For example, deciding between automating a process vis-à-vis the manual process. A differential cost analysis can also be performed where the different relevant costs are compared. This is also known as the relevant cost approach.

Standard Cost

Standard cost is the estimated cost of producing a product or service in the normal course of business. It is also known as target cost. The concept of standard cost is mainly useful for manufacturing organisations. The variance is calculated between the expected cost of an item and the actual cost incurred, and is known as standard costing. It is useful for product costing, decision making and controlling costs but could be time consuming and expensive to implement.

Operating Costs

The fixed and variable costs that are associated with the day-to-day business activities are known as operating costs. They are usually not traced to any one particular product (for example, salaries, utilities, travel and so on). The operating expense ratio reflects on how efficient an organisation is in utilising their costs to generate their sales.

Common Costs

A common cost is a shared cost between two or more departments or users, as it cannot be attributed to a single department or user (for example, connectivity costs). The opposite of common cost is specific cost (where it is directly attributable to the department or user).

Risk-based Costs

These costs may or may not add value to the business as they are based on the risks. Hence, care and precaution need to be vested while incurring such costs. A prudent decision may be arrived at based on the probability of the risk (for example, legal costs).

Investment-based Costs

The costs are usually good to incur, as they guarantee a return on your investment. For example, these may include charges paid to your wealth management consultant (assuming the consultant generates the required return on your investment).

Selling, General And Administrative Costs

These are non-production costs and usually disclosed separately in the P&L statement. These also include costs of support functions, marketing costs, royalty charges and so on. It is best to keep these costs at a minimum, as they do not add any direct value to the production.

Note that some of the costs incurred could have the nature of one or more of the above. For example, a common cost could also be an operating cost.

Why Control Costs?

There are times when the price of your product or service is out of your control (due to industry trends, customs duty, foreign exchange fluctuation and so on). So, if you still want to achieve the desired levels of margins, the best way is to tackle the costs, as they are well within your control.

Let us assess some different ways in which the costs of your business can be optimised with minimal impact on business, and which can contribute towards maximising profits.

Salary

> When SRI had started their venture, they were bootstrapped. So, it was natural that they did not want to spend much, especially on salaries, as it was large expense item. However, over a period of time, they started rewarding their deserving employees with good bonuses, hikes and other perks. This strengthened the loyalty of their best performers and they were ready to give their best for SRI. The three founders further made a conscious decision to provide the rewards only to those who deserved and not standardise it for all employees. Their decision was to be based on performance and no other reasons. SRI was also of the opinion that, "If you pay peanuts, you get monkeys!" So, they wanted to pay good salaries to their deserving employees. However, they were cost conscious as well and wondered how they could create a win-win situation for their organisation and their employees. What are your thoughts on salaries?

For many organisations, especially service-oriented organisations, salaries form a main chunk of expenses. Ideally, salary costs should be directly proportional to your revenue. The higher the number of employees, the more your revenue should increase (accordingly). It will make financial sense to your business only if, with increased salary costs, your revenue also increases. Of course, there will be exceptions (such as when the business is going through a temporary lull).

As an employer, you should be cognisant of how much revenue is being generated per employee. You will agree that, in order to get quality output, the input should be qualitative—and input is usually driven by your employees. It is essential to employ quality people who resonate with your products/services, values and culture of your organisation and, at the same time, are focussed towards contributing to the company's growth. This makes it essential to create a win-win situation not only for yourself but also for your employees, as they should remain motivated and effectively generate revenue for your organisation.

So, before recruiting an employee, SRI prepared a checklist of attributes they wanted from their prospective employees. This was apart from evaluating them on their knowledge, experience and performance levels. They also designed ways and means of attracting the right talent by having many employee-friendly schemes (such as interest-free loans, stock options, performance incentive and so on). Further, SRI made a conscious decision to keep the salary costs slightly low initially but decided on giving good increments based on the employee's performance. Thus, SRI understood that it was an art to strike the right balance between personnel costs and margins.

Suggestions:

- Communicate your expectations to your employees and set their key result areas, which could be a basis to measure their performance.
- Ideally, your support functions (such as administration, HR, and finance departments—the non-revenue generating staff) should be no more than 10 per cent of the total number of employees.
- Set a minimum threshold for the level of revenue per employee to be generated. For example, if there are 10 employees, and you are generating Rs. 500,000 per month. If you are looking to increase your employee strength to 12, you should ensure that your revenue

should then be at least Rs. 600,000 per month (12 * 50,000), if not higher.
- How about employing interns, fresh resources from colleges/universities at junior levels, if they can deliver your requirements, as their costs are usually lesser when compared to experienced personnel?
- To retain your top performing employees, you could also offer them a share of profits or shares in your company.
- You could also offer a percentage of the proven costs saved by the employee or a certain amount if they have contributed towards generating new leads/new revenue for you to sustain their performance levels, and make them want to contribute more towards organisational growth.
- Avoid over-time/shift-based culture, unless it enhances your revenue. Note that over-time labour costs are usually higher than normal costs.
- Analyse the salary variances month-on-month to ensure you are not over-spending or underpaying your employees due to inaccuracies.

> Reflections:
> - *Who are your key staff members?*
> - *Identify back-up options for key employees, should any unforeseen events occur.*
> - *What is your succession plan?*

Labour Mix

SRI's employees' experience ranged from one year to decades' worth. In order to keep costs at an optimal level, SRI's financial advisor checked on their labour mix, as it impacted profits. Are you aware that labour mix can play a role in your business?

> Here is an illustration: SRI has a project to be completed for their client, and is aware that the resource they have identified will be required to work on it for 5 days to complete it. On the sixth day,

> a senior personnel has to check for quality, testing and so on, and fix bugs (if any), so that it can be delivered to the client on the seventh day.
>
> When SRI broke the task down further, they realised that it was a requirement for 5 days by a staff who has around 5 years of work experience. Fresh college graduates or staff with around 2 years of experience would require 7 days to complete the task; a senior resource could complete the task within 3 days. SRI was also aware that the lesser the number of years of experience, the lesser the cost of the resource. If you were the decision-maker at SRI, on what basis would you arrive at which resource you would utilise for this project?

Extrapolate the above example to a larger project, where you need a team of 20 resources to work on the project. What kind of resources would you choose? Fresh graduates or trainees, or interns or resources with mid-level experience or very experienced resources? Probably a mix of resources, after keeping in mind the skills, experience, resource availability, the time of delivery and other relevant factors.

This combination of resources, which you will be deploying in the project, is termed 'labour mix'. It is essential to get the right mix, as it will help you with better margins and efficiency in terms of individual project profitability, thereby contributing to the overall profitability levels of your organisation.

Suggestions:

Some of the criteria with which you will arrive at the right mix can be:

- Cost of the resources and its impact on project profitability.
- Experience and complimentary skill levels of the individual resources.
- Timeframe for task completion.
- A senior member for supervision.
- Impact of the bench cost/idle resources on the organisation.

> **Reflections:**
> - *What is the current labour mix for your existing projects?*
> - *Study the project profitability with different combinations of labour mix while evaluating their skill sets.*
> - *What is the impact of recruiting interns and fresh graduates for some projects versus the cost of training them?*

Recruitment

> As SRI was growing, they required a person to handle their recruitment. An internal person was entrusted with this job alongside his existing role. This person was not keen on taking on the additional responsibility. However, he could not refuse. Therefore, whenever recruitment requirements were handed over to him, he would straight away pass on the requirement to the recruitment vendor—in essence, playing the role of a postman. On the other hand, SRI felt that their current recruitment costs were high and wanted to explore alternatives in order to keep them minimal. How could they go about it? Do you also incur significant recruitment charges?

One of the easiest ways to recruit manpower as per your specific skill set requirements is through the help of recruitment agencies, as they specialise in sourcing your requirements. They usually provide profiles of shortlisted candidates after rounds of interviews which they conduct, thereby saving you the time and effort of browsing through many job portals and profiles. They will charge a fee for their services.

If you are under pressure for profits or have a tight cash flow situation, it may be worthwhile to have other cost-effective options, so that you are not overburdened with additional costs. It is a specific call you need to take. You may decide to fill the positions with your in-house HR team or internal referrals (by other existing employees and so on). However, if you are seeking a niche skill or looking to fill a senior-level position, you may feel it would be better to take help from the external HR agencies.

Another point to help with your decision-making would be to firm up the timeframe within which you want to fill the position, especially if the role is directly linked to increasing your revenue. Note that some HR agencies may seek rights to work exclusively with them, so you need to weigh the pros and cons before you decide on it.

Suggestions:

- If you are filling a position with a HR recruitment agency, negotiate for the best possible terms and conditions. You could also look at a success-based fee.
- You could also fill in clauses to handle situations, such as the consequences of an employee absconding and quitting your organisation within a month, to safeguard your own interests.
- Other cost-effective options include internal referrals by employees (where they are paid a set amount as a token of appreciation so as to incentivise their efforts in finding a suitable person for the organisation).
- If it is a junior position you want to fill, how about advertising in the local newspapers, searching through job portals, or utilising social media effectively, word of mouth via your contacts and so on?
- I have seen instances where both internal referral policies exist and recruitment agencies offer their services—in such cases, you have to ensure there is no duplication of payment for the same person you are recruiting through the agency as well as your existing employee. This problem could also arise if you are working with different HR agencies. You may want to have checks and balances to avoid such ambiguities.
- If you are having a mass recruitment drive, re-negotiate the terms with your recruitment agency.
- Note that, for senior or niche profiles, recruitment agencies might charge a higher premium.
- Place advertisements in low-cost local newspapers for certain positions.
- In the offer letter for employment, be sure to include the requisite notice period an employee has to provide your organisation, and

vice versa in case of separation. Do you want to have the option of buying out the notice period of your prospective employee? You may decide as needed.

> **Reflections:**
> - *What is your organisation's policy if an employee absconds?*
> - *What factors will make it attractive for a person to join your organisation?*
> - *What are the financial elements you will educate the new employees with during the induction programme?*

Ghost Employees

> SRI got to know that one of their friends' organisations had 'ghost employees', which resulted in increased payroll costs. The employers of the other organisation were not aware of the ghost employees for almost 6 months, which resulted in a huge loss. It was unearthed at the time of audit, when the head count did not reconcile with the monthly salary payments. So, SRI wanted to take precautionary actions and did not want ghost employees in their organisation. What should they do to avoid having the occurrence of ghost employees? Have you checked for ghost employees in your business?

As your business grows, the number of your employees is also likely to increase. With the increase in number of employees, you might not be in a position to know each and every employee personally. There could be possibilities of fraud and there may be ghost employees—and, hence, your payroll costs could be inflated and falsified.

As a hypothetical example, let us assume that you have just bagged a new contract and you anticipate around 50 new employees to join. In reality, only 48 people may have been recruited, and the remaining 2 employees may be shown in employment records but not recruited. As the 2 are ghost employees, records for recruitment, identification, bank accounts and so on could be provided but the fact remains that they do not exist physically. It may not be possible for you to monitor such instances on a case-to-case basis. So, you need to be watchful of this. It is wiser to introduce internal controls that are likely to prevent such occurrences.

Suggestions:

- You could introduce biometrics to enter and exit the office, which is linked to the employees' unique employee identification number.
- If you have the system of timesheets, you may reconcile the monthly timesheets with your payroll register.
- You could also resort to job rotation amongst your employees.
- Segregate the roles of recruitment, approval for open positions and decision-making.
- Scrutinise the monthly payroll variance report.
- Conduct surprise random checks for employees across different verticals/different locations.
- If you smell something fishy, forewarn your auditors to pay special attention or to investigate in the specific area in depth.

Reflections:

- *List the possibilities of having ghost employees in your organisation.*
- *Apart from the above-mentioned points, how else can you prevent the occurrence of having ghost employees?*
- *Who from your team can be made responsible to independently monitor such ghost employees?*

Outsourcing

During one of SRI's growth spurts, the founders were promised by one of their clients about a potential new business opportunity, which meant that SRI required 10 new resources exclusively for this activity. SRI was faced with a dilemma as to whether it was better to hire employees on a contractual basis or to outsource employees for this project. SRI wanted to know which option would be beneficial to implement. Have you evaluated hiring contract staff/outsourcing staff for your business?

WHAT THE FINANCE

Outsourcing is a practice in which an individual/company performs tasks, provides services or manufactures products for another company. It is a method of evaluating a particular process that can be done in-house versus getting it done outside. Outsourcing has its pros and cons, and advantages can vary based on specifications.

Contracting employees means that they are not considered permanent staff. They are usually hired for a particular period or a particular project, after which their association with the organisation ends. If required, they can be re-hired thereafter or at a much later date for another project. They can be hired either from manpower supplying agencies, recruitment agencies or directly. These employees are usually not given benefits that a regular/full-time employee is given (such as PF, gratuity, leave salary and so on).

Outsourcing or contracting employees usually happens when:

- There is a lack of in-house specialisation or expertise.
- When it is cheaper to outsource.
- When there is an urgent timeframe to be met.
- When you do not want to retain employees after a particular period (and incur salary costs and bench costs).
- A part of the project is not an area where you want to focus upon/is outside your scope of growth and so on.

Based on your requirements, weigh the alternatives between outsourcing and having the service in house.

In the above example, SRI decided to employ the 10 resources—it made better business sense for them to employ these resources, as they could save on costs and also utilise them in other newer projects which were expected thereafter.

Another example: SRI wanted the team to focus fully on the growth of their business, and therefore decided that areas such as housekeeping, office security and so on were not areas they wanted the team to spend their energies on. Hence, they decided to outsource it to experts who specialised in that area. They were cognisant that, sometimes, it may work out to be more expensive but felt it was better to outsource, as they did not want to be bothered with the associated repercussions (such as replacement of the office boy and so on).

Contracting of employees, especially from other companies for specific skill sets, may prove more expensive. SRI realised that, if they were to recruit a person as their employee on rolls, they had to pay Rs. 50,000 per month. On the other hand, if they outsourced it, the amount they would have to pay the outsourcing company could be Rs. 80,000. While prima facie it made sense to hire the person as an employee, they looked at it on the longer term. The requirement of the specific skill set would last for only 4 months; thereafter, they did not have a need for the person. So, they realised that if they were to have a full-time employee, they would incur bench costs (expenses for keeping a non-revenue generating employee). Even if SRI were to terminate the employment contract, they would have to incur notice period charges. So, if you are in a similar situation, make a suitable decision after weighing all the options.

Suggestions:

- You may want to do partial outsourcing—for example, you may want to hire an in-house admin supervisor to supervise outsourced housekeeping staff.
- Evaluate the benefits between a short-term contractual employee and a permanent employee.
- Ensure the legal terms and conditions, legal provisions (such as payment terms, termination clause, notice period, provision to convert the contract employee into a full-time employee and so on) of the outsourcing/contractual employees are in place.
- Remember to insert a specific clause with the recruitment agency (if required), that you have the right to recruit an outsourced person into your organisation (after paying the agreed recruitment fee) at a later date.
- Also, state the termination period and termination clause clearly in the contracts (either outsourcing or contractual employees).
- If required, enter into a non-disclosure agreement with the outsourcing company/contractual employee.
- You may also want to have interns/fresh graduates for certain jobs

as they might not be as expensive as an experienced person.
- You could also have talented personnel from tier-2 and tier-3 cities, if they fit your requirements.

> **Reflections:**
> - *What are the possible areas in which you can explore outsourcing options?*
> - *What would be the advantages and disadvantages of outsourcing for your business?*
> - *How would you handle the reactions towards outsourcing from your current team?*

Time Cost

When SRI's financial advisor mentioned to them that time spent is also a cost and that it should also be considered while arriving at pricing, SRI could not comprehend the concept. Do you know how to calculate the time cost of your business?

The concept is primarily applicable to the services industry. While labour cost is included, time cost is usually ignored, probably because it does not have a specific 'cost' to it in terms of cash outflow. However, what you need to remember is that time is money and, therefore, efficient and effective utilisation of time will be rewarding either in terms of maximising revenues (by contributing to increased production or service) or in minimising costs (in terms of man-hours spent and the associated costs thereon).

It is also important to arrive at the right hourly charge-out rate per hour. This varies based on the knowledge and experience of each resource. The higher the knowledge and experience, the higher the hourly rate. This is usually arrived at after taking into account the average salary, overheads incurred and amount to be retained towards profit. This also plays a role in arriving at the pricing of a particular project.

Example 1: SRI has bagged a contract for Rs. 10 lakhs, to undertake product development that has to be delivered in 2 months. The actual time taken to complete this project was 3 months. The extra time taken of 1 month is the time cost. In terms of numbers, it translates to one month's salary costs, production loss of another project and other related overheads in terms of the project. This also meant that it could eventually run into project loss. Further, it could potentially impact the subsequent project that was planned for the third month, which is also the cost of opportunity lost.

Example 2: SRI has to quote for a particular project. The total time estimated to complete the project is as follows:

Delivery head – 1 hour (Charge-out rate per hour – Rs. 10,000): Rs.10,000

Quality head – 3 hours (Charge-out rate per hour – Rs. 7,000): Rs. 21,000

5 Supervisors – 5 hours per supervisor (Charge-out rate per hour – Rs. 5,000): Rs. 125,000

3 Team Leads – 20 hours (Charge-out rate per hour – Rs. 3,000): Rs. 180,000

3 Trainees – 30 hours (Charge-out rate per hour – Rs. 1,000): Rs. 90,000

Total estimated time cost: Rs. 426,000

Based on the estimated time cost, SRI can quote a suitable amount to their client. It can be slightly higher after including the margin if required (and the final price can be arrived at depending on market rates, clients payment capacity, margin for negotiation and so on).

Suggestions:

- While bidding for projects or arriving at the pricing, remember that time is also a cost.

- If required, you may want to include the time spent by you (the business owner) on certain projects where you can directly relate/identify the time spent by you on it.
- Compute charge-out rates for your team based on their experience and level of expertise/specialisation while arriving at the pricing for a contract.
- Keep a close watch on the time spent. A good way to do this is to introduce and automate timesheet mechanisms, which will help keep track of the time spent.
- Whenever you sense the possibility of a cost overrun, mitigate the further extra hours that may be spent on that particular project.
- Avoid, if possible, over-time charges for the time over-run.
- If the project is delayed due to a delay from the clients' side, negotiate with the client and get these costs covered. The best way to overcome this would be to state it clearly in the contract at the time of signing, so that you do not have to incur these costs.
- While bidding for contracts, keep some leeway for the time over-run in order to keep your loss of profit at minimum levels.
- If you are operating on a time-and-material basis with the client, this may not be applicable. It is, in a way, a safe model as you are assured of the revenue that is proportionate to the time spent. However, ensure that the client agrees to the time you are charging for the particular project.
- I have encountered instances wherein the completion of projects is prolonged. This impacts not only postponement of your income but also proportional increase in costs for the relevant time period. Hence, it is prudent to ensure that projects are completed in a timely manner.

> **Reflections:**
> - *What is your mechanism to track the time spent on each project?*
> - *What controls exist to prevent manipulation of time?*
> - *Who is monitoring the project wise time clocked and taking necessary actions, if required? What is the time cost of time spent by you?*

Idle Resources

> During the course of their business, SRI realised that they had idle resources and capacity and wondered if that could be utilised in any manner. Do you also have idle resources that are not utilised to their full potential?
>
> There were instances when some of SRI resources remained idle, such as during the time gap between the finishing of one project and starting of the next. During this time, their employees were found in shopping malls or in the movie theatres, which annoyed the founders. Another instance was in the case of new machinery, which SRI was operating only at 50 per cent of its capacity—in the remaining time, it was kept idle.
>
> In both the aforesaid instances, SRI will incur costs irrespective of the idle time. It will be salaries in the case of manpower and depreciation, maintenance charges and so on in the case of equipment. How do you handle such situations?

What can you do as the business owner to obtain the most out of such circumstances? You have to look for ways and means to effectively utilise the idle resources/idle capacity in such a manner that your losses are curtailed.

Your decision should be based on the duration of the idle resources and capacity. If it is for a short-term, you need to think of effective ways of utilising them for that period. However if the idleness were going to be for a longer term, you would need to take a quick, prudent business decision. You can weigh the pros and cons on a case-to-case basis and take appropriate decisions.

Suggestions:

- Seek alternate deployment of idle manpower for short-term needs such as research and development activities or learning and development activities.
- Alternatively, you could upgrade their skills by sending them for specific training sessions.

- If required, this time can also be used for knowledge transfer between resources.
- Regarding the machine/equipment that is kept idle, evaluate options of generating extra revenue from them. For example, renting it out to someone who requires such services.
- If it makes sense to produce/utilise some quantity in advance with the help of the machine/equipment, incorporate that as well in order to avoid over-utilising it when business growth surges.

> **Reflections:**
> - *What is your current idle capacity?*
> - *What is an acceptable amount of idle capacity for your business, according to you?*
> - *What are the pros and cons of effectively utilising idle capacity?*

Rework Costs

> The quality control team at SRI was pressed for time as they were chasing many deadlines at the same time. To make it worse, a couple of team members were on leave due to sickness and personal emergencies. To meet the deadlines and due to stress, the quality team overlooked certain aspects, which proved to be costly, as it required rework. SRI was incurring additional costs due to rework and was strongly advised by the Board to avoid incurring such costs. What can they do? Do you incur rework costs in your business, too?

If the quality of delivery does not meet the specifications of the customer, not only are rework costs incurred but your brand name and the reputation of your organisation is also tarnished—and this impacts future orders of the business. Hence, it is best to ensure the highest quality of delivery right from the beginning. It may also be wise to check periodically with the client if the delivery is in line with their requirements (if you are delivering in batches).

However, there could be instances when, for various reasons (such as lack of understanding of the customer requirements, change in specifications by the client, quality of the product, damages and so on), there could be situations were rework is warranted. At such times, the costs related to rework are incurred. These costs could be in the form of salaries for resources, direct overheads related to the project and indirect overheads, as well as loss of opportunity arising from not completing other projects.

The consequences of rework costs are quite similar to the time cost overrun, as rework costs translate to extra time cost.

Suggestions:

- Keep a constant watch on the quality of delivery.
- Do regular periodic checks/sample testing on quality.
- If possible, negotiate an extra amount with the client for the rework costs incurred.
- For other suggestions, refer to related suggestions under 'Time cost'.
- On certain projects, if you think there is a possibility of rework, it is better to provide a cost on a conservative basis in the same financial period as, otherwise, the margins of the future period are impacted.

Reflections:

- *How will you ensure that rework costs are nil or kept at a bare minimum?*
- *Who is monitoring the quality of delivery?*
- *What is the way you can recover the rework costs, should they be incurred?*

Rent

When SRI had started their operations, they worked out of a small apartment were Ram was staying. Within a few months, as they started to expand, they realised that they required a proper office

> space to function. So, they rented an office premise. Within a year of operating in the office space, the rental cost increased in line with the local market. Further, they required more office space as they were expanding rapidly. At the same time, they wanted to spend a minimal amount on fixed overheads such as rent. SRI wanted to know how to optimise the office rental cost, especially since it formed a substantial part of their fixed cost. Do you have an office space for which you pay rent?

For many organisations, it is essential to have an office premise, and office rental is a clear fixed overhead that eats into your profits. Apart from rental costs, there are also other associated costs such as maintenance of premises, energy costs, wear and tear, and so on.

The larger the premises, the higher the rental cost and related costs. However, for some organisations, it may be vital to showcase a plush office—this is a call that each individual organisation has to make. Let us see some ways in which we can ensure optimal utilisation of space.

SRI managed to remodel their existing premise in a cost-efficient manner and moved on with their challenge of balancing the cost and space. This enabled them to become more space efficient

Suggestions:

- If you have an efficient office planner or architect, seek their ideas for space optimisation.
- If a training room/boardroom is mandatory, evaluate options of converting the same room for either purposes (assuming both rooms will not be required at the same time).
- Preferably, enter into the rental lease without a lock-in period.
- Ensure that the lease terms are in line with the current market conditions of your location.
- For maximum space utilisation, weigh the options of working on a shift basis.
- Assess options of co-working spaces.
- If it is worthwhile, you may want to evaluate tier-2/tier-3 cities, where rental costs are lower. The outskirts of the city may also offer lesser rentals. However, if it is not conducive, do not opt for them.

- Ensure that the space occupied by each workstation, cafeteria, restrooms, lobby, pathways and so on are utilised optimally.
- Partitions/collapsible doors may also prove to be a good option for effectively utilising the available space.
- Before entering into the lease, negotiate hard with the lessor to enable you to get the best deal.
- Remember, if you are using brokers to help you identify the premises, you will need to incur brokerage expenses, too.
- Proximity, accessibility, quality of the premises and so on could be some of the parameters you may want to evaluate.
- In anticipation of future growth, do not block your funds in large premises. Do not get extra space until you are absolutely sure of the new business. Do the groundwork and shortlist the premises so that, once you get the new business, you can occupy the new premises.
- Some small start-ups prefer to hire a huge apartment that serves as both home and office space. This may work for you, too, but evaluate the pros and cons of this option first.
- If you deem it fit, you can provide a flexible/work-from-home options for your team, thereby minimising the need for office space.
- Remember that the rental deposit that you have to pay (usually around 6 months of rent in advance) has an impact on your cash flow.
- If you are using your own premises as office space, you can charge the expense to your business and claim tax benefit. However, the rent your business pays you will be taxed in your individual capacity.

Reflections:

- *What happens if you do not have a specific office premises to work from?*
- *What are the factors that influence the location of your office premises?*
- *How will you know the current market rental rates for the location of your office?*

Energy Cost

> The location where SRI's office was situated faced frequent power outages, resulting in high voltage fluctuations. This resulted in not only their work getting disruptive but also damaged their IT equipment. Hence, SRI ensured that their office had constant power back-up. This meant that their energy costs were higher. Considering the prevalent power shortage from their place of operations, SRI also wanted to explore ways to keep their energy costs minimal. If you have such concerns, what are the alternatives you can consider?

Energy costs refers to the costs incurred in generating, distributing or converting one form of energy (electrical, mechanical, chemical, thermal and so on) into another. It includes both monetary and non-monetary costs (environmental impact).

All businesses invariably incur power costs (unless you are in the power generating business, these costs are direct fixed overheads). Power shortages also cause a surge in the costs, in the form of generator running expenses, wind energy and so on. In some instances, energy cost is the basic driver of production and, depending on the power requirements (or shortage), it can play a role in arriving at pricing as well. Under such circumstances, a cost-benefit analysis of procuring energy versus not having sufficient energy to sustain production needs to be weighed.

As a business owner, it is only wise that you keep these costs at a bare minimum—you cannot do away with these costs, as they are essential in your day-to-day operations of your business. Hence, it is best to ensure that you conserve and sustain energy as an internal policy within your organisation, thereby reducing the impact on the environment and keeping your costs at a minimum as well.

Suggestions:
- Develop an organisational culture along the lines of saving energy. You could also put up posters reminding the employees of the same.

- Conduct periodic energy audits (if your energy expenses form a substantial amount of the expenses) to ensure the energy is utilised effectively and that there are no leakages.
- Ensure regular maintenance and periodic checks of functioning of equipment such as generators, to get the maximum yield.
- In times of power shortage/power cuts, resort to alternate forms of energy (such as windmill energy), which is likely to down bring your costs, as against running a generator.
- If your business is often operating after hours (especially some high-energy consuming equipment), check if such a measure is absolutely essential or look for alternatives.
- If you own a data centre within the premises, ensure that the temperature is maintained at the right level to prevent excessive energy consumption.
- You could opt for LED light fittings that consume lesser energy. They are ideal for the long term, as they consume less power (but they do cost more than regular light fittings).
- Alternatively (if you are okay with incurring a higher one-time cost), you could install automated lights (especially in rest rooms and other less frequented areas).
- A word of caution: If you are procuring diesel, beware of possible fraud between the quantity purchased and the quantity consumed.
- If you are moving to a new office space (especially in the outskirts of the city), check on the availability of power (or else, adjust your budgeted costs accordingly if you need to purchase additional power).

Reflections:

- *How do you monitor your energy cost consumption?*
- *Identify one of your employees to monitor the energy consumption, including the common area charges.*
- *How will your employees be made aware of your energy cost consumption policy?*

Maintenance Cost

> SRI engaged a business coach, and they were involved in dissecting each expense item to evaluate the value derived by incurring each of the expense. One such expense item that caught their attention was the annual maintenance costs. SRI had been paying for these costs on a yearly basis for most of their equipment, but hardly ever utilised the services. SRI felt it would have been better to spend on such maintenance costs on an individual basis rather than opt for the annual charges. What do you think? Have you also entered into Annual Maintenance Contracts (AMCs)?

As the name suggests, these expenses are incurred on an annual basis for maintenance work that is undertaken. It could pertain to maintenance of computers, air conditioners and so on.

While it is essential that all equipment need to be serviced periodically for better performance, you need to weigh the consequences of incurring these charges on a case-to-case basis. To illustrate, weigh the consequences of not entering into an AMC as against entering into one. Understand the services rendered in each AMC. While some AMCs may be for periodic maintenance, others could be for immediate preference given for you as a customer in case of repair. Hence, you have to decide on a case-to-case basis.

Obviously, for crucial/older equipment it may be wiser to opt for an AMC. A call needs to be taken based on the importance and working condition of the equipment. Further, calculate the financial impact of entering into an AMC as against the one-time charges incurred to undertake any sort of repairs and/or maintenance.

Of course, the one-time charges will be high when compared to regular maintenance. However, the frequency of incurring the one-time charge will be the differentiating factor in deciding between the two.

Further, note that the expenses incurred will have to be apportioned between 2 financial years if they pertain to different financial years.

For example, let us say the AMC cost for an equipment of SRI is Rs. 12,000 per annum and is it effective from the July 1 of a particular year. As SRI's financial year is from April to March, the amount to be charged as an expense in the current financial year is for the nine-month period from July to March. So, the charge for the current year would be Rs. 9,000; the remaining charge of Rs. 3,000 will be incurred in the next financial year (for the period April to June).

Suggestions:

- At the time of purchasing the equipment, you can try to negotiate for a free one- (or two-) year maintenance of the equipment.
- Regular checks are to be conducted on the functioning of the equipment.
- Preventive maintenance needs to be undertaken wherever possible.
- If you have a specific administration department, they can take charge of the maintenance aspects (i.e., internal maintenance who can handle period checks, preventive maintenance and so on).
- Do a cost-benefit analysis between the AMC cost and the frequency of the one-time cost.
- If the expense is spilling over into the next year, remember to include it in your budgeted expenses for the next year.
- Also, note that the impact on your cash flow will be immediate/as soon as you enter into the AMC.

Reflections:

- *What are the consequences if you do not have an AMC for specific equipment?*
- *How will you know when some equipment's AMC is due to be renewed?*
- *What makes it worthwhile to continue using the old equipment with an AMC? Compare with buying a new one.*

Purchases

> SRI had many items to purchase for their business, and wanted to know how to make effective purchases—about which they asked their business coach. By performing a detailed scrutiny, the business coach pointed out the differences in the purchase rates of a simple, yet regular item: Toilet paper. SRI was purchasing toilet paper from different vendors and from different brands, as per their requirement. However, when they analysed it, they figured that they had paid varied prices for the same thing. They extrapolated the same for their other purchases, too, and realised how they had to streamline their purchase process. What are all the purchases you make for your business and how would you streamline them?

The purchases for your organisation can range from stationary to computers, raw materials to professional services. The items that are to be purchased depend on the nature of your industry, and ultimately boil down to the decision that you want to take on the items that you want to buy for your business.

It would be a good discipline to issue a Purchase Order (PO) for all purchases (especially big-ticket items). A Goods Received Note (GRN) can be issued when the items procured are received. It indicates the items purchased, quantity, terms and conditions of purchase, credit period (if any) or advance payment made, agreed price, delivery terms, applicable taxes and so on. A PO acts as a binding contract between the buyer and the seller.

As a standard internal policy, you could set out a purchase policy that clearly states the procedure for purchase within your organisation. It can also specify the internal approvals to be obtained, items that can be purchased, approved list of vendors, payment terms and so on. The policy should also state details about the persons authorised to sign the PO on behalf of the organisation.

Suggestions:

- While making high-value purchases, it would be good to obtain 3 or 4 comparative quotes, which will help you to distinguish the price points and services offered.
- Try to negotiate the price, ask for free additional services or get a cash discount (if you are cash-rich).
- You can also check for free installation or services (where applicable) for certain time periods with your supplier.
- If possible, source your requirements from the manufacturer or the wholesaler, where usually the prices are relatively lesser.
- Try not to agree to 100 per cent advance payment terms, as it could get difficult for you to subsequently have a hold on your delivery and installation.
- Let your PO state all the terms and conditions (such as whether the agreed price is inclusive of taxes, the validity of the PO, delivery date, credit period, exact product specifications and so on).
- If the online purchase is cost effective, opt for it. However, do check where to go for subsequent repairs and maintenance and so on.
- Be on the lookout for festive discounts, coupons, season special and so on.
- Maintain a goods inward (and outward) register to keep track of the items that come into your premises (and also the ones that are exiting).
- If your purchases are not in line with your order, ensure that you return them and get them replaced.
- For any foreign purchases, check with your finance person on the applicability of import duty credits, duty drawback, withholding tax impact and so on.

Reflections:

- *Explore the various cost-effective sources for purchases.*
- *Who is monitoring the quality and quantity of the items purchased?*
- *How will a slight delay in your purchase impact your business?*

Amortisation

> When SRI prepared their initial budget for the year, they had not factored in amortisation, nor did they provide for it in their monthly financials. After their books were audited, they were surprised to know that it affected their P&L statement. Did you know about it? This further caused a bit of embarrassment in front of their Board members, as one of the items causing the difference between the budgeted numbers and actual numbers was due to amortisation.

Amortisation is a method of spreading the payments over a period of time (usually over a few years). Be it amortisation of expenses, amortisation of loans or amortisation of assets, the impact on the P&L is spread over the years.

Expenses that can be amortised include pre-incorporation expenses, pre-operative expenses and so on. These include expenses that were incurred just at the start of the business but the benefit of which is obtained over the years. For example, costs incurred by SRI in setting up of the business can be split in the P&L for over a five-year period. This helps in spreading the costs so that there is no huge impact on the P&L in one particular year.

Amortisation of loan refers to when the principal part of the loan is paid over the life of the loan, in line with the amortisation schedule, usually by the Equated Monthly Instalments (EMI) wherein the interest component is repaid before the principal is paid and reduced. Readymade spreadsheets are available to compute this. Note that EMI impacts cash flow and the interest component impacts the P&L.

Amortisation of assets refers to allocating the cost of an intangible asset (such as intellectual property, patents, trademarks and so on) over the asset's estimated useful economic life. The main difference between amortisation and depreciation is that amortisation pertains to writing off of the cost of intangible assets whereas depreciation is for tangible assets.

Therefore, in principal, amortisation eats away at your profits, as it is an expense, even though there may not be a physical cash outflow.

Suggestions:

- Understand and evaluate the impact on the margin each year while using amortisation. Remember to include amortisation in your budget.
- Check, with the help of your chartered accountant, the impact on income tax through amortisation.
- If it is beneficial, you can add it towards your tax planning.
- You could amortise expenses such as pre-incorporation expenses and amortise intangible expenses.
- Determine the ideal period to spread the amortised expenses. Bear in mind that it has to also make logical sense and also be in line with reality.
- If your organisation is working on a shift basis, the higher will be the rate of depreciation as the number of working hours will be higher.
- Remember that amortisation does not impact your cash flow.

> **Reflections:**
>
> - *What is the ideal period for each class of asset/expense for amortisation?*
> - *What are the pros and cons of amortising relevant item?*
> - *What are your possible tax benefits in each case of amortisation?*

Capex vs. Opex

> During SRI's audit, their auditors distinguished between capital expenditure and operating expenditure, which affected their profits. In order to save their rental costs SRI had modified some of the office furniture and also procured new furniture to accommodate more workstations. SRI capitalised the entire amount as capital expenditure. However, their auditors' contention was that only new furniture should be capitalised and that the cost of modification and alteration was to be expensed as operating expenses. Are you aware of the difference between the two?

Expenditure incurred towards purchase of any assets such as computers, land, building, software, vehicles, equipment and so on are known as capital expenditure or 'capex'. 'Opex' or operating expenditure is incurred for the day-to-day operations and is also known as operational expenses. They are short-term and usually ongoing in nature.

Opex impacts your P&L right away by diminishing your profits to that extent. Capex impacts your cash flow immediately as your bank balance reduces by the amount of purchase. The impact of capex on P&L is usually staggered because of depreciation.

In the above instance, the amount spent by SRI on modifications was operating expense in nature, as it was required for the smooth running of the business; the new furniture procured was capital in nature and hence capitalised.

Here is another illustration to help you understand better. SRI purchased a laptop for Rs. 60,000. As they had paid for it, their bank balance was reduced by that amount. However, in their P&L, the impact was subject to their depreciation policy. Their depreciation policy was to depreciate assets over 3 years—therefore, the impact on their P&L was Rs. 20,000 over 3 years. On the other hand, if their depreciation policy was to depreciate assets over 4 years, the impact on their P&L would be Rs. 15,000 over 4 years.

You may argue that you want to fix the depreciation of the computer over 20 years (then, the impact in P&L is only Rs. 3,000 each year). The number of years of depreciation should be a reasonable and realistic one. You know that you cannot expect a computer to last you 20 years! So, fix the depreciation policy accordingly. You are free to have different depreciation rates for various classes of assets. For example, while you may depreciate a car over, say, 5 years, you may depreciate your furniture and fittings over 10 years. Bear in mind that you cannot keep changing the depreciation rates year-on-year to suit your convenience. However, over several years, you are allowed to change depreciation rates to reflect the real picture.

Yet another way to decide on capex versus opex is to evaluate the financing options of lease versus buy. By opting for a lease, the asset is financed by the lease option, and you do not own the asset. It is an option where you are renting the asset and it is thus an opex item. So, you do not incur related asset costs such as maintenance costs and also no huge down payment amounts. The other option is to buy (which is a capex item) wherein you purchase the asset and you are the owner. You can either pay the entire amount or take a loan to fund the purchase. You may decide based on your requirements.

Suggestions:

- Remember that opex impacts your P&L in the current year and Capex impacts it over a period of few years. Depending on your requirement, it also enables you to decide between a lease or buying option.
- Depreciate assets over realistic period of time.
- If you are unsure about the depreciation period over the life of the asset, refer to the income tax depreciation rates. You can use it as a benchmark to arrive at your depreciation rates.
- Remember to account for depreciation on a month-on-month basis.
- If, for instance, you have purchased the asset on December 15, and your financial year ends on March 31, the depreciation impact in the current year will be for 3.5 months.
- If the asset is sold before it is fully depreciated, the difference between the selling price and the book value of the asset is to be recognised as profit or loss on the sale of the asset.
- If the asset is damaged or lost during the life of the asset, the book value of the asset remaining in the books will be written-off and shown as loss of asset.
- It is good to have your assets insured.

Reflections:

- *What is the return on investment for your capex?*
- *What will be the impact on your revenue with the capex purchased?*
- *Weigh the tax benefits between opex and capex on a case-to-case basis.*

Retainer Model

SRI had heard about the retainer model through their friend, but didn't know what it was. When they got to know about it, they wanted to create a win-win situation from the retainer model. Do you know what it is and how it could help your business?

Retainer fee is a cost that is incurred upfront in order to pay the services of professionals such as legal service providers, consultants, freelancers and so on, who are usually engaged to perform certain specific actions on your behalf.

> Look at this example. SRI does not have an in-house legal team and requires the services of a legal consultant. SRI is aware that they require legal opinions for preparing and vetting their customer contracts, employee contracts, rental agreements, preparing non-disclosure agreements and so on. Apart from this routine work, they also anticipate that they would need to seek legal advice on other issues revolving around your business operations like investor agreement, supplier agreement etc. So, they have approached ABC lawyers.
>
> ABC lawyers can charge SRI a fee for each service provided, based on the time they spend. Let's say this is at an average of Rs. 5,000 per hour. An alternative given to SRI was to pay a flat fee of Rs. 20,000 per month for utilising their services for up to 10 hours each month—anything over and above the 10 hours would be charged at Rs. 3,000 per hour. In other words, even if SRI does not utilise their services in a particular month, they have to pay Rs. 20,000. For utilising their services up to 10 man-hours in a month, SRI incurs only Rs. 20,000. On the contrary, if SRI did not have a retainer fee, then for 10 hours, SRI will incur Rs. 50,000.
>
> Therefore, your decision to opt for this model would depend on the frequency of requirement of such services in order to gain the most of it.

If you are in the business of providing services to your customers or regular maintenance, you could provide the retainer model to your clients. This will help you with steady monthly revenue.

Suggestions:

- Make a realistic requirement of the quantum of usage of such services.
- Obtain a quote from the service provider for both options.
- Compare and compute your costs under both methods.
- Choose the one that is more economical for your purpose.
- Payments can also be negotiated and customised for project-based payments to your vendors.
- If you are planning to render a retainer fee option to your customers, calculate and provide your rates to your customers/potential customers. You could also position yourself to be a strategic partner with your customer, and thereby ensure a long-term customer relationship.

> Reflections:
> - *Identify the services required, which could warrant a retainer fee.*
> - *What are the benefits of retainer versus having the service in-house?*
> - *Explore the various possibilities for you to offer a retainer model to your customers.*

Travel Cost

As part of their cost control measures, SRI was exploring options to keep travel costs at a minimum. What would be the potential areas they could look into?

> One of SRI's employees, who was in charge of business development, had undertaken a business trip. As part of entertaining a prospective client, he incurred high entertainment expenses. This was not usually the culture at SRI. Further, Sid later

> got to know that the prospective client who was entertained was actually a childhood friend of the employee's, and hence did not permit this amount to be reimbursed.
>
> There was yet another situation when one of their senior managers who was on a business trip in another country suffered a mild heart attack. Thankfully, he was treated immediately and doctors gave a green signal for him to fly back. The senior managers' wife had to be flown in due to this emergency. The doctors had advised the employee to lie down as much as possible to avoid any possible strain—so, the employee was flown in business class (although, as per policy, he was entitled only to economy class travel). His wife also accompanied him in business class during the return journey. This was an exceptional situation. As the heart attack happened during a business trip, on humanitarian grounds, SRI agreed to pay for the wife's travel.
>
> However the finance team in SRI which was in charge of making the payment, raised a question as to how the wife was entitled to fly back on business class and insisted on specific approvals, thus creating unpleasantness with the senior manager. As Isha approved the wife's business travel, the finance department paid for it.
>
> While the senior manager complained about the finance team not being compassionate, Isha was glad that the finance team had followed the company's policies of getting specific approvals for any exceptions.

Travel costs forms part of the expense—however, travel may sometimes be an essential part of the business, thereby making it necessary to exclude this cost item. Travel includes all forms of travel, such as by air, train, bus and so on. It also includes mileage reimbursement, cab reimbursement and so on paid to staff.

In order to avoid ambiguity in travel, it is always better to lay out clear terms and conditions. Hence, a comprehensive travel policy stating internal travel rules and regulations on the organisation's travel policy is needed. Further, approval procedures, approval limits, allowances and so on need to be stated clearly in the travel policy. This will help to avoid confusion, and the employees can adhere to the given policies and procedures. (Also refer to example on Page 21.)

Suggestions:

- Plan your travel in advance if possible, and book the tickets at the earliest to get the best fares.
- If the travel pertains to a customer's cause, include the travel cost in your price or charge it back to the client as out-of-pocket expenses. Ensure that the contract with the client clearly specifies that the out-of-pocket expenses will be recharged to the client.
- If business class travel is permitted, specify the terms and conditions when it can be undertaken.
- Set limits per kilometre if the employee is using his own transport for business purposes.
- Ascertain if the travel is absolutely essential (especially if you are on cost-saving mode) or if the matter can be resolved over phone or video conferencing.
- Set proper approval limits, reimbursement policies, per-diem allowances, accommodation limits/approved hotels in your travel policy to avoid any unambiguous situations.
- Ensure sufficient travel safety precautions for women associates.

> Reflections:
> - *Weigh the benefits of incurring each travel.*
> - *What are the best ways to get the best deals in accommodation, foreign exchange and so on?*
> - *What is your travel insurance policy?*

Economies of Scale

When Sid attended a seminar, he got to hear about economies of scale and wondered how to achieve and capitalise on economies of scale for SRI. How relevant is it for your business?

WHAT THE FINANCE

When the quantity of production or service is increased and is performed on a large-scale basis, it results in lowered average variable costs—this is known as economies of scale. This provides a cost advantage, as the fixed cost per unit decreases when the volumes are higher. However, 'diseconomies of scale' kicks in when the volumes go beyond a certain number. As an organisation grows and increases its top line, it has a better chance to decrease its costs.

> Here is an example: Let us assume that the cost of support functions (such as admin, HR, Finance, IT and so on) at SRI is Rs. 200,000 per month, and the turnover is Rs. 2,000,000 per month. Currently, the support cost is 10 per cent of the turnover. Assuming new orders are obtained, the turnover of the organisation doubles to Rs. 4,000,000 per month, but the cost of the support function still remains at Rs. 20,000 per month (which is now 5 per cent of the turnover). SRI can sustain with the same level of support cost till it reaches a turnover of, say, Rs. 8,000,000 per month. If the turnover exceeds Rs. 8,000,000 per month, SRI may need to employ additional support resources to handle the higher volumes of transactions, the decision of which may be taken at the appropriate time or when nearing such increased volumes.

Based on this concept, you can apply the logic in other areas of costs as well including logistics costs, transportation costs, material costs and so on.

Suggestions:

- As the business owner, you need to learn to optimise and arrive at the right levels of economies of scale for each function.
- Examine your technical aspects (such as production process) by improving the operating efficiency of the business process.
- If your team is working on a project, evaluate the manpower cost versus the revenue from that project to arrive at the optimal levels to gain from economies of scale.
- This principle is also applicable while negotiating for prices on your purchases, where you can get volume-based discounts.
- You can also achieve managerial economies of scale by investing

in the right levels of expertise in line with the growth of your organisation.
- Financial economies of scale tick in with the growth of the organisation, as there are more assets that can be offered as a collateral and lower interest rates. It is a similar case with marketing and brand building.
- With a larger customer base, you can spread across your fixed costs, thereby reducing the cost per unit.

> Reflections:
> - *Which areas of your business can you apply the principle of economies of scale to?*
> - *What will be the benefit of implementing the same?*
> - *Assess any risk involved in applying economies of scale.*

Hidden Cost

> During the course of their operations, SRI realised that they had opted to seek some professional secretarial services to prepare and maintain the documents such as minutes and also run around and meet the government authorities. The hourly charges quoted seemed reasonable, but the invoice showed a much higher amount. SRI did not know the associated costs that came with it as it was not told to them upfront. So when the secretarial agency charged them for the time that was spent on waiting to meet the authorities, travel time, and so on, SRI was put off. However, when they closely looked at the contract with the agency, it did not specify that they would be charging SRI for such items. Isha, being vigilant about such matters, ensured that SRI was not over charged. What about you? Have your scrutinised your books for hidden costs?

Are you aware of the different hidden charges that your business incurs? Hidden costs could be in the form of wastage of resources, recurring charges, costs that may not provide any value-add and so on. They are sometimes costs that are charged over and above the purchase price (a common example is during the purchase of an air ticket online).

A thorough internal audit by the concerned stakeholder may reveal specific potential areas of such hidden costs or leakages in the system. Proactive measures could help in curbing such unwanted expenses to ensure that the margins are not eaten into.

SRI had incurred the hidden charges in the form of silent debits by the bank. Upon negotiation with their bankers, SRI was able to minimise such charges for the future. Other hidden costs could include wastage of resources—a small cost initially but a larger associated cost later on, which you need to be watchful of.

Suggestions:

- Firstly, unearth the hidden cost in each function.
- Understand the terms and conditions involved in each transaction, as you will become more aware of such implications.
- During the negotiation stage, you could check on the possible hidden charges (if any).
- Conduct periodic scrutiny of bank statements to check on any silent debits by the bank.
- Engaging in periodic, in-depth analysis of the resources utilised and to explore any potential savings.
- Scrutinise agreements and understand the terms and conditions on any hidden costs stated in them, prior to signing the agreements.
- Be alert and aware of the potential vulnerable business areas such as minimising production costs, production time and so on, which can help in discovering probable hidden costs.

> **Reflections:**
> - *What are the vulnerable areas of your business, which might have hidden costs?*
> - *What measures can you take to curb them?*
> - *Who can help you unearth the hidden costs?*

Introduction Fees

> SRI was seeking investors to grow their business. Once, they were approached by an agent who offered to introduce them to potential investors, in exchange for a commission as a percentage of the amount they would obtain. In your opinion, do you think SRI should proceed in accepting their offer? Are you also in a similar situation?

There are some agents who charge a commission on the pretext of introducing potential investors or customers. This commission is called an 'introduction fee', and is the charge for introducing you to your potential investor.

While I agree that it could be essential and also tempting to get potential investors who can fund the business, or even when given a lead to a good customer, the principle of 'Caveat Emptor' prevails—this means that the buyer should beware.

Therefore, you need to ensure the authenticity of such agents and watch out so that you do not fall prey to such tempting propositions.

Suggestions:

- Verify the background of such agents, as well as of the potential investor and customer leads.
- Seek references from other successful referrals, if required.
- Watch out for false promises—only when the payment is received is the deal real.
- Word your legal agreement accordingly.
- Negotiate and agree on a success-based fee rather than blindly agreeing to a flat fee.
- It may be better to negotiate the fee as a percentage of the investment/business order so that you are aware of the margin that you will be generating from the particular project.
- Ensure that you make the payment to the agent only after you have received the funds from the potential investor/potential customer.

> **Reflections:**
> - *What is your purpose in seeking the assistance of such agents?*
> - *What will happen if you do not get the investment from the potential investor the agent is referring you to?*
> - *How important is it for you to obtain the potential lead from the agent? What other sources do you have to generate leads?*

Automation

> SRI wanted to automate their routine processes. Considering that SRI was relatively a young enterprise, would it really be beneficial to automate at this juncture for their operations? Thus, the trio had to perform an analysis of whether SRI should opt for automation or not, specifically listing down the advantages and disadvantages. By giving weightage to each point and also prioritising the requirements, SRI concluded that it was not the right time for them to venture into such an activity and that they would require automation in 2 years' time. Have your considered automation for your business?

Automation is the technique whereby a process or system or equipment operates automatically, with minimal human intervention.

In this modern age of technology, everyone would like automation, as it is meant to save time and cost, and also enhances the effectiveness of the processes. It is further meant to reduce human error, increased safety, higher efficiency and so on. On the flip side, it also means a large initial investment, lesser versatility, unforeseen costs due to automation, higher unemployment and so on.

There are also areas such as robotic accounting that are gaining popularity. Explore the relevant areas of automation that may be suitable to your business operations.

For you to decide between automation versus manual, do a cost-benefit analysis by comparing the cost of automation to the cost of human intervention, time saved, increase in production (or service) and related benefits of each.

Suggestions:

- While evaluating automation, remember that you do not have to follow it just because your friends or others in the industry have been doing it.
- Perform an independent analysis of it to arrive at your results, as no one else will know your business as well as you.
- Evaluate the loss of jobs that automation will bring about.
- Are you in a position to provide alternate roles for those employees within your organisation on account of automation?

> **Reflections:**
> - *What will be the impact of automation on your business?*
> - *What areas can be automated?*
> - *Perform a cost-benefit analysis that automation can bring to your business.*

If you are cautious about managing your expenses and make sure you spend right, you can work to maximise your profits. It also involves discipline in your approach and having the right decision-making ability towards your expenses. This is bound to get better with the experience you gain over the period of time.

Now, for you to meet all your expenses, you need to have sufficient funds in the bank and manage the funds efficiently as well. So, let us now look at ways and means of how you can ably handle the funds of your business.

Chapter 5

WHAT IS IN YOUR BANK

As entrepreneurs, I am sure you would agree that, "Cash is king!" The amount of funds you have in the bank determines all cash outflow, as cash outflow is dependent on your cash inflow. As entrepreneurs, at times, you may be challenged by your cash situation. Some entrepreneurs I spoke to, mentioned how they had sleepless nights wondering about how they would manage to pay their current month's salaries and so on. If you plan your cash properly, this can be a very easy task.

There have been many well-known companies in the past that have filed for bankruptcy, such as American Apparels. Some of the reasons why American Apparels went bankrupt included continued losses, rising legal fees (due to illegal immigrants and sexual harassment cases), high debts and controversial branding. While it is not uncommon for businesses to get into financial crises, lack of timely action exacerbates the problem.

With better planning, you can protect yourself from the cash crunch. Given that your product or service is doing well, I am sharing, in the next few topics, some tips on how you can focus better on your cash situation and ensure that you are well prepared.

Another common mistake some entrepreneurs tend to make is to plan their cash spend based on their bank statement balance. By doing so, you might miss on the cheques issued but not yet cleared, cheques in transit and so on. This could have major implications, especially during times of cash crunch, and I am sure you do not want your cheques to bounce on account of this. So, beware of this.

Cash Flow Projection

> Although SRI's business was flourishing, they perpetually faced a cash crisis. This was because of many reasons, such as not collecting their dues on time, not properly managing their funds, lack of coordination amongst themselves in handling payments, not keeping proper track of their receipts and payments and so on. However, they were not able to identify these issues and so did not know what was wrong. The three of them did not realise what actions needed to be taken to correct the situation, as their focus was mainly on the business operations. The founders felt that the onus of cash was only on their accountant, who was handling their payments. Also, they failed to educate their staff on the importance of timely action to rectify the cash situation. SRI never had a clue about what receipts and payments were due and when. These are common issues faced by many entrepreneurs. Are you also one of those who thinks that the onus of cash management is not on you?

As a first step, you need to understand the sources and utilisation of your cash. Hence, a cash flow projection has to be prepared. Cash flow projection (also a cash flow budget) is the statement of cash flow for a future period, reflecting the anticipated cash inflows and outflows for a certain period of time. Usually, the period is for a year. However weekly, monthly or quarterly cash flow projections can also be prepared. This helps in determining the cash requirements. Anticipated cash surplus or cash deficit can be planned for accordingly. Cash flow projection is also known as cash flow forecast.

Preparing the cash flow projection is essential in order to anticipate the cash requirements for the business to survive. Further, it also helps in knowing the company's affordability in terms of paying the suppliers, vendors and employees. It acts as a forewarning before the business runs out of cash.

As this is a futuristic statement, this is prepared based on expectations. However, for best and accurate results, the projected cash inflows and outflows must be on a realistic basis.

WHAT THE FINANCE

SRI was advised to get into the habit of preparing monthly cash flow statements and reviewing the same. A sample cash flow projection is given below:

Cash flow projection of SRI Ventures for a six-month period ending June 20XX (in INR)

Particulars	Months					
	Jan	Feb	Mar	Apr	May	Jun
Opening balance	50,000	2,59,000	1,39,000	38,000	-37,000	-28,000
Receipts						
Cash sales	10,000	7,000	5,000	8,000	5,000	6,000
Receivables from Customer A	1,50,000	–	1,00,000	2,00,000	90,000	1,50,000
Receivables from Customer B	60,000	50,000	30,000	20,000	50,000	80,000
Receivables from Customer C	2,50,000	75,000	1,25,000	3,50,000	1,80,000	2,00,000
Interest earned	5,000	12,000	7,000	2,000	–	–
Scrap sale	–	–	–	10,000	–	–
Total cash available	5,25,000	4,03,000	4,06,000	6,28,000	2,88,000	4,08,000
Payments						
Salaries	2,00,000	2,00,000	2,00,000	2,00,000	2,00,000	2,00,000
Bonus	–	–	–	2,00,000	–	–
Rent	30,000	30,000	30,000	30,000	30,000	30,000
Electricity	5,000	5,000	5,000	5,000	5,000	5,000
Insurance	–	–	75,000	–	–	–
Office supplies	7,000	7,000	7,000	7,000	7,000	7,000
Repairs and maintenance	2,000	2,000	5,000	2,000	2,000	5,000
Travel	4,000	5,000	4,000	5,000	4,000	5,000
Connectivity costs	3,000	3,000	3,000	3,000	3,000	3,000
Purchase of fixed asset	–	–	–	2,00,000	–	–
Professional fees	10,000	10,000	10,000	10,000	10,000	10,000
Audit fees	–	–	–	–	50,000	–
Income tax payments	–	–	25,000	–	–	25,000
Miscellaneous	5,000	2,000	4,000	3,000	5,000	2,000
Total cash required	2,66,000	2,64,000	3,68,000	6,65,000	3,16,000	2,92,000
Closing balance	2,59,000	1,39,000	38,000	(37,000)	(28,000)	1,16,000

This statement is meant to provide a comprehensive view of the expected cash status.

As is evident from the above example, although, at the end of June, the cash situation is positive, it is negative in the months of April and May. Therefore, better cash planning is required so as to not run into a cash deficit. In the above example, the purchase of the fixed asset could probably be postponed to the next couple of months. Alternatively, a bank overdraft or similar facilities can be obtained to tide over the temporary cash situation.

Monitor your fund position regularly to gain better visibility. You can have a pie chart representing where the bulk of your cash is being consumed, what percentage of your total outflow is towards which spend and so on. Similarly, your cash inflow can also be broken down into various customers, various segments or various verticals for you to know how your cash is being generated.

> Reflections:
> - *What are the payouts that can be postponed to a later date?*
> - *How can your business sustain itself with regard to the cash from your own operations?*
> - *What is the way to speed up your dues?*

Advance From Customers

> During SRI's audit, their auditors noticed that SRI did not take any advance from customers. Further, the time taken to raise an invoice and collection thereafter seemed to take a long time. As a result, their working capital was blocked for a longer time, thus resulting in cash shortages for SRI. Does your capital also get blocked? Do you take an advance from your customers?

As a best practice, it is always wise to take an advance from your customer as an upfront payment before you commence working on their assignments/

project. The amount of advance can be 100 per cent, 50 per cent or even 10 per cent. It may vary according to several factors, including negotiations with your customer, the delivery period, delivery schedule, cash position, working capital requirement, rapport with your customer and so on.

If it is a new customer, for instance, it is always better to get a higher advance. Even if it is an older/regular customer, if you are customising the product/rendering exclusive service for him/her, it is always better to obtain a full advance or a significant portion as advance. If you do not want an advance (for whatever reasons), have a back-up plan in place for the items that your prospective customer could reject. Ask yourself what you would do with those products that were exclusively customised for the particular customer, and mitigate your losses arising thereon.

I remember, we had once appointed an event manager for organising a particular event. Without collecting an advance, she started organising the event and incurred expenses. Unfortunately, the event had to be cancelled. Since there was no advance given and the agreement did not mention anything, the event manager was not paid. This example is to caution you about consequences when an advance is not obtained.

Remember to account for the advance received in your books and collect the remaining amount upon final delivery or completion of the work as the case maybe.

You can also agree to receive a partial advance, as per the various stages of completion of the work done of the assigned project, so that your working capital is not impacted.

Reflections:

- *What would the impact be on your working capital if an advance were not taken?*
- *How can you negotiate better with your customers for getting an advance?*
- *What is your business policy if the customer pays you an advance but cancels the contract and seeks a refund?*

Status of Receivables

> The auditors observed that SRI did not have the practice of following up on their dues. SRI did not take an advance, completed the work, delayed raising an invoice and thereafter did not take action to collect their dues. When probed as to why no action was taken, they realised that no one internally took responsibility of reviewing receivables and following up for the payments. In fact, one of their invoices from a customer was due for over two-and-a-half years as no one had checked if the amount was paid or not. Further, no one in SRI knew when an invoice was due for payment as it was not being monitored.
>
> SRI realised that one of the reasons for this state of affairs was because the teams worked in silos. They seemed to lack transparency in the work front and there was no formal way to communicate between teams, thus resulting in the delayed collection and follow up process of their receivables. How do you keep tab of your receivables and get timely payments?

One of the reasons some entities face a cash crunch despite making book profits is because of the status of their receivables. If your collections do not happen on time, your cash inflow is affected and, therefore, there is a good chance that you will face a cash flow deficit.

In the course of my interaction with some entrepreneurs, I was told that, in the businesses that run on credit, the follow-up on receivables sometimes does not happen on time and, as a result, they sometimes face a fund shortage. One of the best ways to follow up would be by systematically tracking the collection report periodically. The age analysis of your debtors reveals the position of your receivables.

Go by your industry norm with regard to the credit period that you would like to provide your customers. Let us say it is 60 days from the date of your invoice. Therefore,

- As a first step, ensure that you raise the invoice on time (as soon as the product is delivered or service is rendered).

- Mention in the invoice the credit period for ease of reference. You can also choose to opt for the due date on the invoice.
- If required, you can send periodic reminders to your customer (say, at the end of 30 days). Prepare a checklist or set reminders to help you follow up regularly.
- If, even after the given credit period, you have not received your payment, follow up regularly either through emails or phone calls to get the expected date of payment.
- If you are doubtful about recovering the amount (for whatever reasons), you will have to provide for bad debts in your book and write it off after 3 years (if it is still not recovered). Whenever the amount is received, it can be brought back into the books.
- It is always advisable to ensure that there is an interest clause on delayed payments in the contract with your customers. You have an option to choose whether to activate it or not, but it is always favourable to mention this clause to be safe.
- Note that a delay in collection of receivables causes blocking of working capital.
- If required, appoint debt collection agencies for better collection and improved liquidity.

A sample of the age analysis of SRI is given below:

in '000s

Customer	0 to 30 days	30 to 60 days	60 to 90 days	90 to 120 days	120 to 150 days	150 to 180 days	over 180 days	Total	Comments
X	80	90	85				95	350	Resolving dispute on the outstanding invoice over 6 months. Collection likely during next month.
Y		75	85	60				220	Customer to make the payment next month

Z						160		160	Customer in cash crunch. Has promised to pay next week.
Total	80	165	170	60	0	160	95	**730**	

Compute your debtors turnover ratio. The formula is:

$$\text{Debtors Turnover ratio} = \frac{\text{Accounts receivable}}{\text{Average sales per day}}$$

Alternatively, it can also be calculated by accounts receivable divided by [annual sales/365] to arrive at the number of debtor days in a year, as illustrated below.

In the example above, if the annual sales were Rs. 1.46 crores,

$$\text{Debtors days} = \frac{730{,}000}{1{,}46{,}00{,}000/365} = 18.25 \text{ days}$$

Based on this formula, you can calculate and track the performance of your debtors.

> **Reflections:**
> - *What does your debtors turnover ratio reveal about your collection cycle?*
> - *How can you create a robust collection system in your organisation?*
> - *Who is in charge from your team to follow up for dues?*

Bad Debts

> As we are aware, SRI does not have the habit of following up regularly for their dues. They had not followed up on their dues from one of their customers, who eventually went bankrupt and

> hence did not pay SRI. The amount that was due to SRI was written off as bad debts. SRI regretted not having taken timely action to collect their dues and learnt their lesson in a painful manner. What should you do in order to avoid having bad debts?

When the amount that is owed in exchange for the services rendered or the product that has been purchased from you is not received beyond the given credit period, and your customer does not intend to pay you the money, it is known as a bad debt. So, it is in your own business interest to ensure that there are no bad debts incurred.

Normally, when you still have not recovered the amount due from your customers for over a period of time (say over one year) and the recovery seems doubtful, you provide for bad debts. Should you receive the amount subsequently, you reverse the provision for bad debt. If the amount is still not recovered over 3 years, you write it off. However, if you receive the amount after writing it off, you can disclose the amount as other income. Check on the tax implications with your consultant.

The following steps can act as a useful measure in bad debt collection:

- As a first step, ensure that your accounts receivable status reflects the correct status.
- Remember that the older the age of the debt, the more difficult is the collection.
- Hence, as soon as an amount becomes due, start following up with your customers through phone calls, emails, formal letters and so on.
- If you have not received your dues despite umpteen follow-ups, appoint a legal consultant to write demand letters.
- If giving a minor discount to the customer will help the cause (as it is better to forego a small amount rather than the entire debt), do that.
- Come to a consensus with your debtor and agree on a debt recovery plan.
- If you are still unable to recover the debt, appoint a collection agent who can collect on your behalf.

- If none of the above works, you will have to go to court to recover your dues.

As prevention is better than cure, it is always better to take sufficient precautions to ensure that your dues do not become bad. Try the following:

- Develop an effective payment policy and adhere to it to the maximum extent possible.
- Review your credit terms. Sometimes, long credit periods prove difficult for recovery.
- Offer cash discounts to your customers for upfront payments.
- Obtain advances from your customer whenever possible.
- Better to be safe than sorry. Hence, ensure robust collection systems should be in place in your organisation.
- Remember that legal action will increase your costs further.

> Reflections:
> - *What will act as an alarm for you to follow up your dues?*
> - *What are the preventive steps you can take to avoid bad debts?*
> - *How will you handle a customer who is dilly dallying in paying the dues?*

Credit Facility

> Due to their cash crunch, SRI wanted to explore the option of how credit facility could aid their cash situation. SRI's payables were soaring and so were their receivables. They felt overwhelmed looking at the payables and thought that by opting for credit, they would be able to pay off their dues. They did not think of following up strongly on the monies owed to them, as they were not used to chasing payments and found it hard to ask their customers to pay up. Hence, they wanted to opt for the credit facility. Have you looked at getting credit facility for your business?

Many times, business organisations face cash crunch situations. They may be making profits in the books but yet remain low on cash. This happens if your debts or dues are not collected on time. At the same time, you have to pay your monthly salaries and pay your suppliers and vendors as per the due date.

So, as a responsible business owner, you have to plan your cash diligently and ensure that you are not stuck in a situation where you are facing a cash shortage, especially due to lack of planning for your cash requirements.

Please note that, while cash inflow is not fully in your control, your cash outflow is within your means. Hence, apart from planning your cash outflow, you can also opt for a credit facility to aid you with your cash flow situation. Credit can be taken either from the bank (as an overdraft), moneylender, vendors, or family and friends, to help you manage this short-term cash flow crisis. Banks or moneylenders are likely to ask you for collateral security to safeguard their own interest. However, most importantly, note that a credit facility warrants additional costs in the form of interest cost.

Here are few pointers that you can work on:

- Negotiate on the best rates of interest on the credit facility that is being offered to you.
- Even if the loan is from extended family or friends, enter into a simple loan agreement.
- State the term of the loan, terms of repayment, rate of interest and so on, clearly in the agreement.
- Repay the loan at the earliest to minimise the interest costs. Note that interest costs eat away into your profits.
- One way of managing the cash outflow would be to specifically state in the agreements with the vendors on the credit period. Get the maximum credit period that would be beneficial for you. For example, you can state that all the bills will be paid within 60 days of receiving the invoice (*not the date of the invoice*) from the vendor. You will have to specifically negotiate on this period with each vendor. This can help in reducing your interest costs.

- Contrary to the above, when you have excess cash at your disposal and want to pay off some of the vendors earlier than the due date, negotiate for a cash discount, thereby lowering your costs.
- Periodically (say, at the beginning of each month), prepare the cash flow forecast so as to know your requirement for each month, which will help you to plan accordingly.
- One of the entrepreneurs I spoke to specifically mentioned about having 3 months' worth staff salary in the bank as a buffer, especially for rainy business days.

> **Reflections:**
> - *Who are the persons you can approach for a short-term business credit facility?*
> - *What are the plans of repayment of such credit?*
> - *How will the credit help your business? For what period of time will it help?*

Debt vs. Equity

> As SRI's business was expanding, they required more funds towards their growth and increased working capital requirements. SRI could source their requirements either from investment (through promoters or other investors) or from their retained earnings. The options of getting the funds could either be as debt or as equity. What are your growth plans, and how will you match your fund requirements?

To put in simple terms, debt is a form of a loan, wherein you borrow funds from a bank, financial institution, commercial finance companies and so on, to run your business. On the other hand, equity is sharing the ownership of the business with the investors or partners who fund your business in the form of capital, expecting your business to make profits in the future.

Each of these options has its advantages and disadvantages. It is best to weigh your individual pros and cons before deciding the option best suited for your business.

Some of the main advantages of debt financing are:

- You continue to be the owner of the business.
- You can run your business the way you want.
- Easier to obtain when compared to equity.
- You have the opportunity to grow your business (at a cost).
- The interest payments are usually eligible for tax deductions.
- Lender does not have any claim on the profits of the business (unless agreed otherwise).

The flip side of debt financing is:

- Has an impact on the cash flow, as the debt needs to be repaid.
- The interest cost on the debt reduces your profit.
- Collateral needs to be provided to secure the loan.
- If your debts are not repaid within the timelines, your business assets (or, failing which, your personal assets) could be at stake.
- If the repayments are not made as per the agreed timelines, it has an adverse impact on your credit worthiness.

Main advantages of equity financing:

- No repayment until sufficient profits are generated (subject to the investor selling his stake).
- No interest cost and, therefore, no impact on profits.
- A less risky option as you do not stand to lose business (or personal) assets.
- The investors can contribute to mentoring your business growth.
- Your loan history is usually not mandatory for equity financing.

The flip side of equity financing:

- By diluting the ownership, your stake as the owner reduces.
- Important business decisions have to be taken in consultation with the investors and there could be the possibility of difference of opinions.

- You have to share your profits with the investors.
- The only way to end the relationship with your investor is to buy him out (which would usually be at a higher price).
- It may not be easy to find the right investor to match your working style, thought process, sharing your vision, growth strategy and so on.
- If at all your commitment for dividends is not met, the relationship with the investors could turn sour.

Therefore, based on the above factors, you can decide on the option that is well suited to your specific requirements.

> **Reflections:**
> - *How will you utilise the extra funds that you have received either through debt or equity?*
> - *What makes it worthwhile to get the funds, either as debt or as equity?*
> - *From your perspective, which one (debt or equity) has a better advantage for your business?*

Book Profit vs. Cash Profit

> SRI was operating at very good margins and had good profits as per their audited financials. However, they were facing a cash crunch and were struggling to make timely payments to their vendors. They failed to understand why this was happening and hence requested their financial consultant to explain it to them. The consultant pointed out instances as to why this was happening and advised that the best way for SRI was to follow their cash situation on a regular basis in order to avoid cash crunches. Have you ever wondered why cash profit is different from book profit?

You need to understand the difference between cash profit and book profit. As an entrepreneur, both are important for you. Book profit is often different from cash profit. Under both methods, the transactions considered are the same, yet cash profit is different from book profit.

As the name suggests, cash profit is profit in terms of cash only. It does not take into account the non-cash items such as depreciation, provisions, prepayments, outstanding payables, receivables and so on. The profit as per this method is purely in terms of the cash. Note that all cash receipts are not immediate revenue (for example, a customer could be paying you an advance). This helps with your cash flow but it is not book profit until the revenue is recognised.

Book profit, on the other hand, takes into account all the transactions, irrespective of whether you have made the payment or not, whether you have received the payment or not, and also takes into account all the non-cash items such as depreciation. This is based on the accrual method of accounting.

As an entrepreneur, cash profit is important because you require the cash to run your day-to-day operations of your business, repay your loan and so on. However, for accounting purposes, book profit is what is considered.

Note that the income tax is computed on your book profits. Your audited financials reflect the book profit. Hence, computing the book profit is important.

> Reflections:
> - *Reconcile the difference between your cash profit and book profit for better understanding.*
> - *What do the above numbers reveal about your business?*
> - *What do you think you need to do to improve both?*

Pitching to Prospective Investors

> SRI decided to scale up their business in and penetrate foreign markets, as they believed it had good growth opportunities for them. So, SRI decided to seek angel investors for their business. They were unsure as to how to go about pitching to their prospective investors. What should they be doing? Have you also been thinking about raising funds through angel investors?

Apart from being confident, assertive and fluent in your pitch, it would also be good to reach out to as many potential investors as possible. Here are some guidelines to follow when you are pitching to your potential investors.

- Keep it short and simple.
- Usually, the initial few minutes are crucial, as the investors make up their minds/form an opinion about your pitch.
- Be crisp and focussed.
- Give a brief about your product or service, and state the greater purpose.
- Give a background on the leadership team.
- Mention any awards, recognition won or any grants obtained.
- Mention about your board members/business advisors, if any.
- Make it interesting for them to hear your story and your journey so far.
- Talk about the financial journey till now.
- Highlight the USP (unique selling point) of your business.
- Share about product-based market analysis/market share and marketing strategy.
- Talk about the market your business is catering to (B2B, B2C, target audience and so on).
- Elaborate on your business model and revenue generation.
- Speak about growth and scalability.
- Association with domain champions/experienced persons.
- Tell them as to why yours is a great business to invest in.
- Tell them about your plan of action of utilising the funds obtained.
- Update them about your other investors, if any.

By taking into account the above-mentioned points, you should be in a position to get a better idea of the financial performance of your business. I am leaving you with some reflections to ponder upon so as to gear yourself up better.

> **Reflections:**
> - *Who can help you in managing the finance journey of your business?*
> - *What will motivate you to look forward to measure your financial performance?*
> - *How will you get a better level of financial comfort of your business?*

I suppose you now have a better understanding of managing your funds, and you are also more aware of the importance of handling your cash situation more effectively and efficiently.

Now that you know the elements you need to look into for better cash management, let us move on to another important aspect of managing a business. It is the compliance aspect, wherein we will look into the various applicable compliances of your business. The objective is to make you mindful about the compliance aspects, as the cost of not being compliant to applicable rules and regulations is very high. You might as well go through the rigmarole of the compliance rather than being non-compliant.

Chapter 6

WHAT TO WATCH OUT FOR

This section highlights the importance of adhering to compliance. As the business owner, you are in charge of ensuring that you comply with the necessary rules and regulations. So, there are few aspects you need to be watchful of.

With regard to compliance matters, there should be absolutely no compromise. It is extremely important to adhere to the compliance aspects as per the specified rules and regulations, as applicable to your organisation. While the cost of compliance may not have a major financial impact, the cost of non-compliance is high. Apart from penalties, interest charges and so on, it could sometimes also result in imprisonment (depending on the nature of non-compliance). Further, you could lose out on funding opportunities due to non-compliance issues. I believe it is better to be safe than sorry—hence, I am providing some generic tips on issues that you need to be compliant with, irrespective of the nature of your business venture.

Compliance issues could be a challenge in itself. The only suggestion is to adhere to compliance. Be aware that the rules keep changing and, hence, be abreast of the latest compliances that are applicable to your business. As an entrepreneur, you need to be aware of such matters. You can always get them implemented through your auditors or other professional agencies offering such services. But remember that the onus is on you.

Over to a bird's eye view of compliance matters.

Basics in Place

> When Sid, Ram and Isha were starting their business venture, they were unclear on the requisites. They did some groundwork (such as networking with other entrepreneurs, seeking advice from experts, speaking to consultants and so on) to understand the various things that were required to get their entity registered. Do you know all that is required for your business?

Depending on the type of legal entity (sole-proprietorship, partnership, Limited Liability Partnership or LLP, Limited Company and so on) of your business, check on the basic legal documentation and registrations that need to be in place. You may also be required to register your organisation under applicable laws (such as GST registration).

Some examples of the above include (but not limited to) having:

- PAN (Permanent Account Number)
- TAN (Tax deduction and collection Account)
- GSTIN (Goods and Service Tax Identification Number)
- GST (Goods and Services Tax) Number
- Bank account
- Digital signature
- Directors Identification Number (DIN)
- Licence under Shops and Establishment Act
- Applicability of Provident Fund, Employee State Insurance and so on

Also required could be a Certificate of Incorporation, Articles of Association, Memorandum of Association, Partnership Deed, and so on, depending on the type of business.

The above are mere pointers. Please check on the exact applicability for your organisation.

Filing Returns

> At the end of SRI's first year of operations, the trio were not aware that they had to file income tax returns for SRI. They were clueless about the fact that they had to file income tax returns for their business when they had started off as entrepreneurs. SRI started filing income tax returns only from third year of its inception. You thought you were the only one who did not know about this? As this is fairly common among many of the new entrepreneurs, this point finds a place in this book.

Note that even if you have incurred a loss, you have to file your income tax returns. Please be aware of the due dates and submit your returns well before the due date. You have the option to file the tax returns online.

Remember to deduct tax at source (TDS) from the applicable payments to your vendors at the applicable rates and file TDS returns.

If you are registered for GST, you will have to file periodic GST returns as well.

If tax returns are not filed within the due date, loss from business cannot be carried forward for income tax purposes.

Regulations

> There are umpteen laws that exist, and regulations that are required to be adhered to. SRI did not have any clue about them and how to go about it. They felt lost in the ocean of regulations. Do you know how to be compliant with your industry requirements and applicable regulations?

Out of the many laws and regulations, only some are applicable to your business. Further, the laws keep changing from time to time. As a business owner, you need to focus on your business. Although you may argue that these are irrelevant to you, you need to be aware of what regulations are applicable to your business. Technically, you are not expected to be a master of the applicable laws, rules and regulations. However, you need to be aware of them so that you can gauge the impact of such laws and regulations on your business, and take the right business decisions.

Apart from laws, there are also certain regulations from RBI (Reserve Bank of India), SEBI (Securities & Exchange Board of India) and FDI (Foreign Direct Investment), just to name a few, which may or may not be applicable to your business. Understand the applicable ones for your business from your financial advisor.

As a thumb rule, before committing and entering into any major transaction, it is always best to sound it off with your financial consultant, tax consultant and legal consultant to know the repercussions of such transactions. This will assist you in taking prudent business decisions, and your advisor can guide you with the required formalities.

While the Companies Act, Income tax Act, GST and so on are well known Acts, there are other Acts and laws that you would have to comply with. Business owners are sometimes not even aware of the existence of such laws and their applicability. During your periodic discussions with your financial and legal consultants, it would be good to check and get an understanding of the general commercial laws.

It would also be good to discuss such matters amongst your network of entrepreneurs. A good idea is to invite experts from some of these areas to give you a guest lecture in such areas during your forums, as it will help the audience at large.

Some of the commercial laws include (but not restricted to) the following:

- The Information Technology Act
- Negotiable Instruments Act
- Prevention of Money Laundering
- The Patents Act
- The Copyright Act
- The Trademarks Act
- Micro Small and Medium Enterprises Act
- Data Protection Act (to be implemented)

There are also industry-specific laws that are applicable, such as the Motor Vehicles Act, Food and Safety Standards Act, The Insecticide Act, Mines Act, or Pharmacy Act. Do check for your industry-specific laws that govern your business.

Employment Laws

> One day, SRI received a letter from the wife of a newly married employee, stating that she did not get any money from her husband for running their household. So, she provided her bank account details, and asked SRI to transfer a part of her husband's salary into her bank account. Should SRI adhere to her request? Legally speaking, SRI could get into trouble if they obliged, as SRI was legally liable to pay only their employee. So, as an employer, one should be watchful of the legal obligations and subsequent implications. Similar scenarios may arise during the course of your business—what should you do?

The laws falling under employment require extra special caution and attention as, usually, all the laws favour the employee and you will have to be extra vigilant as an employer. Hence, before framing any rules or internal policies, please be aware of the exact implications of such rules. In case of any doubts, please check with a labour/legal consultant.

If your concern about a particular employment aspect is grey in nature, or if you are in doubt and the amount involved is not too much, try to settle with your employee instead of spending time, effort, energy and money on legal costs.

Not only do you need to be cautious with employees, but also be cautious about framing your internal policy/taking decisions regarding the employment rules. To help you understand better, here's an example.

Let us say the government has suddenly declared a holiday (due to bad weather conditions or in order to commemorate a special day or due to demise of a senior government official) on a working day. This will result in loss of productivity for your organisation. You may want to compensate this by declaring another holiday as a compensatory working day. In cases like this, you have to be watchful, because the labour laws may or may not permit this. You have to understand what the government order (GO) states about the compensation part before you finalise. If you go against the GO, you could be penalised.

Some of the other laws governing the employees, especially with regard the payment of salaries and other eligible include:

- Labour Laws
- Gratuity Act
- Provident Fund Act
- Employee State Insurance Act
- Payment of Bonus Act
- Minimum Wages Act
- Employees Compensation Act
- Equal remuneration Act
- Factories Act
- Shops & Establishment Act
- Apprenticeship Act
- Maternity Benefit Act
- Prevention of Sexual Harassment Act

Please understand the applicability of these acts to your organisation. Also, note that the above is not an exhaustive list.

Companies Act

> SRI was considering converting their business into a company. They didn't know what sort of a company it should be and how to go about it. Have you ever wanted to start your own company?

Companies Act is applicable to all sorts of companies—Public Company, Private Company, One Person Company, Domestic and Foreign Company, Companies not for profit and so on. Depending on the type of company you run, the applicability of the sections and clauses of the Companies Act varies.

Companies Act requires you to maintain many registers, file annual returns and comply with the provisions of the Act. It also requires appointment of Directors, holding of Board Meetings, Annual General Meeting, and so on, the proceedings of which has to be recorded in the minutes register. The financial statements need to be audited and the audited financial statements are to be filed with the Registrar of Companies.

As per the Income Tax Act, income tax, advance tax, minimum alternate tax and so on have to be paid. Transfer pricing regulations, where applicable, need to be adhered to. If you are in the Special Economic Zone (SEZ) or an STPI (Software Technology Parks of India) company, the necessary regulations will apply.

Import Export

> One arm of SRI was in the business of import and export. Initially, SRI carried on with these operations without knowing the repercussions of non-adherence to import and export. SRI was also not aware of some of the new changes that had happened in the import export regulations. Did you know the applicability such regulations? Have you also factored in the impact of the foreign currency fluctuations in your business?

You need to be watchful of the compliance issues relating to import and export, and seek necessary approvals from the Reserve Bank of India and other regulatory bodies.

If you are receiving funds from a foreign entity or foreign investor, there are rules prevailing and regulations to be followed around those as well. Requisite forms and returns are required to be submitted, too. Further, there are policies issued by the government in relation to the Foreign Trade Policy and so on.

Some of the Acts include (but are not limited to)

- Foreign Exchange Management Act (FEMA)
- Import and export regulations
- Foreign Direct Investment (FDI)

- IEC (Importer Exporter Code)
- Rules regarding repatriation of funds
- EXIM (Export Import) Bank Act
- Customs Duty

The idea is to create awareness and exposure that such provisions exist and that you need to be compliant with them should you be into any sort of import/export.

Checklist

> There were many occasions when SRI missed making their tax payments and filing the returns within the due dates. They felt terrible each time it happened, yet had not managed to overcome this challenge. They decided to set it right. In order to streamline this process and get into the discipline, SRI introduced checklists. How about preparing a similar checklist for your business?

There are many due dates and deadlines in each month that need to be adhered to, such as advance tax payment, provident fund payment, due date for filing GST returns, monthly TDS remittances and so on. Due to your routine business work sometimes, you may miss these deadlines, and it could result in interest and penalties charges. It may also occupy a mention in the audit report and could lead to further scrutiny by the taxman, thus giving you unnecessary additional work.

The best way to avoid missing such due dates would be to prepare a monthly checklist so that the important dates are not missed due to oversight, public holiday or a weekend. A sample checklist is shared below:

S.No.	Particulars	January	February	March	April	May	June
1	TDS Payments						
2	TDS Quarterly Return filing						
3	PF Payment & Challan						
4	PF monthly return						
5	ESI Payment & Challan						

6	GST payments							
7	GST Returns							
8	Advance Tax							
9	Income Tax Return							
10	RBI yearly Survey							
11	Central Excise monthly return							
12	Central Excise renewal							
13	Professional Tax Payment							
14	Tax Audit Report							
15	Fixed Assets Insurance							

The respective due dates can be slotted into each of the box. Please note that the above is only an indicative one and is not to be construed as exhaustive.

Tax Evasion vs. Tax Planning

> For one of the past years of SRI's operations, the taxman was scrutinising their books of accounts to check if all the necessary tax payments were made. As it was the first time, the taxman had picked on them, the trio panicked. However, they were assured by their tax consultant that there was no need to panic as SRI's taxes were all well planned and that there was no tax evasion. SRI wondered what the difference between the two terms was. Do you know the difference? Do you plan the tax for your business?

As the name suggests, tax evasion is undertaken with an intention to evade the taxes that are due, whereas tax planning is a method wherein after careful planning, the tax liability is minimised. Thus, tax evasion is illegal whereas tax planning is legally permitted. Tax evasion is also known as tax avoidance. The main differentiating factor between the two is the intent.

Tax planning is an art by which the amount of your tax payment is reduced due to careful and permitted planning, whereby your tax burden is minimised. Your tax consultant will be the best person who can guide you in this area.

It is important to plan your taxes as it helps in reducing your tax payment. It also aids in overall financial planning. Effective tax planning is essential as it helps in reducing the tax liability.

Please note that taxable profit will be different from your actual profit. The difference between the two is usually because of tax adjustments, the allowable and disallowable expenditure from the tax perspective. Therefore, seek assistance from tax experts. Remember that tax evasion leads to huge penalties and interest and could also lead to imprisonment.

Fraud

> One of the office boys employed by SRI, who used to run errands for them, was reimbursed conveyance charges on a weekly basis. His mileage claims and bills were approved by Ram, and reimbursed by the finance team. However, over a period of time, the office boy started to forge Ram's signature on his claims and started claiming too many false reimbursements. This came to light only after several months. SRI immediately took measures to sack him and fix the issue. This incident drew their attention as to how they were vulnerable to frauds. How vigilant are you towards frauds happening in your organisation?

Let us see how you can effectively curtail frauds, thefts and pilferages.

It is a no-brainer that fraud, theft, stock pilferages and so on cause not only moral damage within the organisation but also financial damage by reducing your profits to that extent. As a management team, you need to know how to prevent such events from occurring within the organisation.

Integrity and ethics need to form the core value of your organisational culture. This has to flow from the top. The management should periodically remind the team that integrity and ethics form the main basis of the organisation and that the management values such principles. This message has to be driven across verticals and teams. The message has to be that the management has zero tolerance towards any kind of fraud or theft, and that it might result in immediate termination of employment. You need to lead by example.

Be vigilant of all areas that are vulnerable to fraud and initiate preventive steps so that you do not provide an opportunity to commit fraud.

Some points that you could implement are:

- Brainstorm with the senior team/department heads on the possible areas of fraud. Set up internal control mechanisms that can plug the loopholes of such possibilities.
- Job rotation and job segregation can be done frequently.
- Encourage employees to go on leave periodically so that the employee handling in the job in absentia can smell foul, if any.
- Adopt whistle blower mechanisms as part of the organisational culture. A word of caution: Ensure personal differences or professional prejudices are not used under this pretext.
- Periodically, meet your suppliers, customers, bankers, auditors and so on, and hear their woes (if any). You also build your professional relationships this way.
- If required, you can conduct surprise checks or do a test check in vulnerable areas like petty cash, stock and so on.
- Review your monthly management accounts and look for any strange variances.
- Put up posters on the importance of integrity; mention about it during your team meetings, town halls and other official gatherings.
- Be watchful of any errors in the system.
- Introduce automatic checks and balances within each process.

As mentioned at the start, this section is meant to give you an idea that you need to be compliant with whatever applicable laws, rules and regulations. You need to take further steps and understand what other aspects you need to be complaint with.

From here, we need to move ahead to see what more you can do. In the following section, I am going to equip you with tools and some quick steps that you can resort to in order to make handling your business finance easier.

Get ready!

Chapter 7

WHAT IS YOUR WHY

This section explains a few other aspects that will help you in focussing on your profits as well as minimising your risks. Once you become aware of the purpose behind your financial decisions and actions, your connect with your business finance becomes much better and you will get a better hold of finance.

So, in this section, I will run you through few aspects that will help you take good control of your business from the finance perspective. See which ones are relevant, beneficial and what you can implement in your business. It will also tell you how to keep a tab on your business performance.

The section will also touch upon financial discipline. Unlike financial compliance, these are not mandatory in nature but are extremely beneficial to comply with.

'Discipline' is a word not many people like. However, the way to combat it is to embrace it. That is why you need to know your 'why'. Why is it important to have financial discipline? Seek your answers to your 'why' and these become lot more easy to follow.

By making financial discipline a routine and automating it, you will no longer find it cumbersome. If you have a good support function, entrust it with them so that you can just supervise their work. But remember, even for that, you have to get into the discipline of supervising!

Zero Based Budgeting (ZBB)

Isha read about Zero Based Budgeting or ZBB and liked this concept, and immediately wanted to implement it at SRI's ventures. Do you know what ZBB is? Would you also like to roll it out for your organisation?

ZBB helps to ensure that your costs are kept at a minimum. Once the budgets are firmed up for the following financial year, as a normal business practice, the departments' budgets are usually shared with the respective department heads. This usually sets the precedence for spending for the year under review.

> If you want to take a conservative approach on the expenses of the business, ZBB should be practiced. To illustrate, SRI's annual day celebration budget was Rs. 200,000 for the current year. Just because there is a budget, does that mean that annual day has to be mandatorily celebrated? It is a question that one needs to ask. If the year has been an exceptional year or if the employees need to be motivated, it makes sense to conduct an annual day event. On the contrary, if the business was not doing as well as anticipated, you need to question if it is really required to celebrate the annual day just because it has been budgeted—more so as this expense directly eats into the profits.

Therefore, ZBB starts with a zero base. Just because a cost was incurred in the previous years, does it mandatorily mean it has to be incurred in the current period as well? Hence, all expenses must be justified and analysed for each period by the department head, and a conscious business decision needs to be arrived at.

The advantages of resorting to ZBB within your organisation helps in lowering the costs, offers flexibility in budgets, focuses on the core operations and disciplined execution. On the flip side, sometimes, they can be manipulated to one's advantage and could also create a bias in short-term planning. So, prudence needs to be applied on a case-to-case basis.

Few suggestions on how you can go about ZBB:

- You need to challenge yourself/your team on each of the expense heads, on whether that particular expense needs to be incurred or not.
- Even if there is a particular amount budgeted for an expense, you can ensure that it is not necessary to spend the entire amount.
- If you want to be conservative in you approach, you can set high revenue budgets and stringent cost budgets.
- You may also want to give incentives to your employees to motivate those who can demonstrate contributing towards substantial cost savings to the organisation either by adopting ZBB or by pushing for large cost savings from the budgeted amount.
- Ensure that smooth business operations are not affected as a result of ZBB.
- If you are keen to adopt ZBB, ensure that this is effectively communicated to all the employees and team members.
- Reward employees, if required, at the end of the project when they have managed to control substantial costs for the organisation.

> **Reflections:**
> - *How do you think ZBB can be made effective in your business?*
> - *What is the flipside to implementing ZBB in your organisation?*
> - *What is the possible impact ZBB can have on your business?*

Employee Contracts

> Sid's cousin was employed in SRI. As he was a close relative of the co-founder, SRI did not offer any employment contract. However, after working for few months with SRI, Sid's cousin decided to move on to another organisation for better prospects. He did not serve the normal notice period that was required. SRI could not do much as there was no legal contract between them. How is it in your work place? Are all your employees given employment contracts, wherein terms and conditions are clearly specified?

Irrespective of the fact that you have employed your extended family member or childhood friend or any other person as your employee, the first thing you need to have is a contract of employment with the person, stating all the terms and conditions of employment, their designation, monthly salary, working hours, working days, number of leave days they are entitled to, their roles and responsibilities, benefits they are entitled to and so on. It should also state terms about the termination of the employment and the notice period required by either the employer or the employee, as the case may be.

I insist on this because I understand from some start-ups about how this was overlooked, and the repercussions of the same were felt at a later point in time. Ensure that rolling out of offer letters and acceptance by the new employee is part of your internal recruitment process, so that this important aspect is not bypassed.

Apart from the employment contract, it is also good to have a non-disclosure agreement (NDA) with all your employees as well as vendors' employees. The NDA prohibits them from indulging in certain activities that are against the nature of the business of your organisation.

It is also a good practice to keep a copy of the employees' PAN card, passport, Aadhar or any other government identification for your records. You can also opt for hiring the services of background verification agencies (such as www.matrixbsindia.com).

The employment contract serves as a document of vital importance, should a dispute arise at a future date. Hence, it is essential to have this document in place for all your employees. It should be signed by both the employer and the employee, and both should retain a copy for themselves.

Periodic appraisal letters with revised salary and other details should be provided at the end of each appraisal cycle. This also serves as an audit trail.

> **Reflections:**
> - *What happens if your employee files are lost, say in a fire? What is the back-up in place?*
> - *If a certain key employee has misbehaved in the past and repeats it again, what would you do?*
> - *What is the policy on paying bonus to your employees?*

Agreements with Vendors

> In the initial stages of operations, SRI did not enter into agreements with their service providers. SRI's IT operations were outsourced to Ram's friend's company. Being the IT service provider, the employees of the IT Company had access to SRI's confidential data, and one of their employees who was posted in SRI misused this data—which landed SRI in trouble. However, no legal action could be taken, as there was no agreement between SRI and the IT Company. Are you well protected in your agreements with all your vendors?

Similar to employment contracts, it is a good practice to have agreements with all your major vendors. It is sometimes referred to as a Master Service Agreement (MSA). It is an important document, as it states the terms and conditions of the relationship with your vendor. The agreement also states the kind of services to be rendered or products that will be procured, quantity of the product, terms of delivery, the agreed price and so on.

The document also serves as the basis for both parties to plan their requirement and budget for the price of the product or service. Along with the agreement with the vendor, it is a healthy practice to have a confidentiality agreement in place as well. In the absence of a vendor agreement, it would be difficult to prove anything in the court of law should a dispute arise at a later date.

If it is a one-off vendor, it may be good to have a purchase order so that it acts as a document stating the terms and conditions for the one off transaction. The PO can still be issued to a vendor where the MSA exists as the quantity and nature of transaction may vary time to time if it is a regular vendor.

Last but not the least, get your legal team or consultant to vet the agreement, so that all your risks are mitigated and your interests are well covered.

> Reflections:
> - *How do you think an agreement with the vendor can be of use to your business?*
> - *How will you know if agreements exist with all your vendors?*
> - *Who has the authority to sign the agreements on behalf of your organisation?*

Measuring Financial Performance

> SRI had been growing year on year, in terms or revenue, head count and verticals. The founders wanted to know how to measure their financial performance versus their growth. They wondered what the key performance indicators and growth indicators were and whether it was in sync with the other. They probed as to how they could perform even better, and wanted to benchmark their performance in their industry. Have you had similar thoughts as well?

To measure the financial performance of your entity means to evaluate the financial health of your organisation over a given period of time. It is an indicator of how assets are being used to generate revenues and, thereby, profits.

Some of the key performance indicators (KPI) that help to assess the financial situation are:

- Revenue growth.
- Gross profit (product-/service-/segment-wise—as relevant).

- Net profit.
- Aging of receivables.
- Current ratio (ratio of current assets to current liabilities).
- Debt equity ratio.
- Return on capital employed (ROCE).
- Key business drivers (for example, utilisation levels, production efficiency, capacity maximisation, quality of deliverables and so on, as per your industry parameters).
- Specific drivers (for example, customer service, business development and so on, that are required for your organisation's growth, specific to your industry).

The criteria to set the KPIs is that it should be aligned with the overall goals of the organisation, should be quantifiable for measurement and should be within the purview of control of your organisation. Once these are in place, you can share it internally to the respective departments for action.

While setting the targets for your organisation, ensure they are SMART targets: Specific, Measurable, Achievable, Realistic and Time-bound.

Some of the ways to measure the KPI are by assessing:

- Monthly performance.
- Quarterly performance.
- Year-on-year performance.
- Performance against budget/target.
- Financial ratios (like liquidity ratio, efficiency ratio, leverage ratios and so on).
- Cash flow.
- Benchmarking against the industry standards/competitors.

It is important to measure the financial performance of the organisation, as it is the process that reflects the results of the policies and operations in monetary terms. It also portrays the degree to which the financial objectives of the entity have been accomplished.

KPIs can be fixed for the entire organisation and drilled down to each department and, in turn, to the employees based on their levels of responsibility.

> **Reflections:**
> - *Compare your KPI's with your industry-specific parameters to measure your financial performance.*
> - *Analyse the key cost and operational drivers responsible for the variance in the financial performance for each parameter.*
> - *What are the preventive steps that you have in place to meet your performance targets?*

Asset Turnover Ratio

> Over the course of time, SRI had become an asset-rich organisation. SRI was asked by their consultants as to how high their asset turnover ratio was. SRI did not know about this and decided to check what it was and how it could help them. Do you know about it?

This is applicable mainly for asset-intensive organisations or organisations that intend to invest large amounts in their assets.

Whilst there are many other important ratios, I am giving specific attention to this ratio, as this is an important one, especially if you have or intend deploying large amounts into your assets. This ratio indicates the efficiency with which your organisation is utilising the assets to generate revenue.

$$\text{Asset turnover ratio} = \frac{\text{Sales}}{\text{Average value of assets}}$$

For example, let us assume that the average total of SRI's assets is Rs. 100 crores and it remains unchanged for 3 years.

Revenue:
- Year 1 is Rs. 5 crore
- Year 2 is Rs. 20 crore
- Year 3 is Rs. 45 crore

Asset turnover ratio in year 1 is at 5 per cent, year 2 at 20 per cent and year 3 at 45 per cent. So, the higher the asset turnover ratio, the more it indicates that you are effectively using your assets to generate sales.

It is important to calculate the asset turnover ratio as it reflects on the effectiveness of the utilisation of the assets. You can improve your asset turnover ratio by increasing sales, improving efficiency, selling assets and so on.

> Reflections:
> - *What are your must-have assets?*
> - *What impact does the asset have on increasing your revenue?*
> - *What is the projected efficiency level of the asset in consideration?*

Insurance

> SRI had initially never opted for any sort of insurance, as they viewed it as an additional expense. However, one of their office premises had a short circuit that resulted in a fire. While they were glad that there were no serious mishaps, they immediately opted for insurance. What is your take on insurance for your business?

Insurance is an expense that reduces your profit, yet it is safer to be insured. Insurance is offered on a wide variety of services—from insuring your fixed assets to insuring cash to insuring the liabilities of directors as well as insurance on cyber security. Insurance is also offered against fire, protection against theft and other natural calamities such as tsunami, flood or storm.

So, depending on the nature of your business and your requirement, insurance is a good way to keep your business guarded.

Before procuring an insurance policy (for whichever kind of insurance), obtain quotes from various insurance providers and evaluate not just the cost but also the other features that are in-built in the policy.

Check with the insurance agent on parameters such as the time taken to investigate by the insurance agent, the time taken to receive the insured sum, the extent of coverage of the loss and so on. Understand the formalities that will have to be completed before submitting the claim—for example, the insurance may insist on a copy of the FIR with the Police Department in case of theft.

Comprehend the requirements thoroughly so that, should such an event occur, you are aware of the procedures involved.

> Reflections:
> - *What are the consequences of not opting for insurance?*
> - *What are the vulnerable areas of your business that require insurance?*
> - *What could be the pros and cons of providing medical insurance for your employees?*

Negotiation Skills

> In SRI, while Sid and Ram did not negotiate, Isha was always negotiating at every possible opportunity. During a discussion amongst themselves, Isha pointed out the various negotiations she had carried out in the past year in their favour—even she was also amazed at the significant savings that was gained from the negotiations for SRI. Is negotiation a priority for you?

Negotiation skills are vital for any successful businessperson. Whenever and wherever possible, negotiate to your advantage. There are always many rules and regulations but also note that there are also exceptions to these rules and regulations. Further, there is nothing to lose by trying to negotiate to your advantage.

So, at any given opportunity, negotiate in your favour. Seek freebies if you can. Some areas of negotiations include:

- Suppliers and vendors (for discounts, better rates, terms and so on)
- Customers (encouraging for bulk orders, quicker payment and so on)

- Investors (valuation, equity stake, rate of interest and so on)
- Bankers (for better credit facilities, lesser charges, better rate of interest and so on)
- Service providers (for better terms and conditions, scope for relaxing rules, any extras and so on)

In order to have effective negotiation skills, some of the complimentary skills that you need to have are:

- Good communication skills.
- Excellent interpersonal skills.
- Assertiveness.
- Listening skills.
- Decision-making skills.
- Ethical skills.

As a rule, remember to negotiate in all your deals.

> **Reflections:**
> - *Who can negotiate on your behalf?*
> - *How will you handle the situation if your employees want to negotiate their salaries, working hours and so on with you?*
> - *What will happen if you do not negotiate with your customers and suppliers?*

Legal Consultant

> During their initial years, SRI never realised the importance of having a legal consultant, or even reading all the terms and conditions in a legal document. They learnt this lesson in an expensive manner. In one of the software licence maintenance agreements, which they had accepted and signed, there was a clause that stated that, if the agreement were not terminated by a written notice from SRI, the agreement would remain valid and SRI would have the pay charges for the next 3 years. While signing this agreement, they had overlooked this fact—therefore,

> even though SRI was not utilising this software licence, they had to pay a huge sum. If this agreement had been vetted by a legal consultant on SRI's behalf, they felt they could have reworded this agreement to their advantage. How prepared are you with legal aspects?

While it is not mandatory to have a legal consultant, it is another important aspect that is always better to have, especially if there are matters concerning any possible disputes. If the core of your business is not into legal matters, it is not necessary to have a legal person as a full time employee, as you can always outsource this role.

Alternatively, if you want it in-house, you can club this role with an employee who has the expertise—for example, with the finance person or the HR person if they have suitable qualifications or experience to handle it for you. Or, you can also have a qualified individual freelancing for you.

The message I am trying to get across is that it is always in your interest to safeguard your rights and mitigate all legal risks towards your organisation and you.

In the normal course of business, legal expertise is required in drafting (or vetting) all legal contracts, supplier agreements, employee agreements, patents, trademark, non-disclosure agreements and so on.

Further, before signing any document, please read all the terms and conditions. If in doubt, please check on the consequences and ensure that the risks are mitigated. If you still feel it is a grey area, get your legal consultant to reword it for you in your best interests.

Remember to insert interest clauses in the agreements with your customers if they do not make the payment within the agreed credit period. In the case of violation of the credit period, you have the option to demand the interest or not, depending on the time taken, amount due and, most importantly, the kind of rapport you have with your customer. Note that it could jeopardise your future relationship with the customer. So, while it is good to state it in the agreement (to ensure that you receive your dues on time), you have the option letting go of the interest charges to your customer. It is a call that you can take on a case-to-case basis.

Once a master agreement has been vetted by a legal person, you can use the same as a base with other similar vendors. For example, if the recruitment agreement and the non-disclosure agreements have been vetted for one recruitment vendor, you can use the same template with other recruitment vendors. It is not necessary to get legal clearance for each and every contract of a similar nature. Beware while copying the same template—remember to change the date, name of the vendor, payment terms, credit period and so on, as these may vary from vendor to vendor. Read it in entirety before you sign it.

> Reflections:
> - *What are the specific areas of your business where you require legal consultation?*
> - *What if the same legal consultant is also consulting for your competitor?*
> - *What is the contract period with your legal consultant? Who will vet the agreement with your legal consultant?*

Project Evaluation

> Whenever a new project was received, SRI would immediately accept the project. This was irrespective of whether it was really beneficial or not. SRI felt that, by accepting more projects, they would grow. However, on a case-to-case evaluation, they realised that this was not true and that they needed to pick the right projects only and not anything and everything that came their way. What is your attitude? Do you evaluate your new projects?

As soon as you receive a new project proposal from an existing client or a prospective client, it is good to evaluate the project first.

You need to calculate the best and worst case scenarios of the project, and your final decision to accept the project or otherwise would be dependent on the outcome of the valuation. Project evaluation could sometimes be a non-technical one, too.

Once SRI decided to make a conscious call on evaluating projects, they adhered to their policy of obtaining the minimum margin, failing which they would not undertake the project. The exception to this was to be made by a consensus (for example, a CSR activity or a prestigious client, or if there was any other mileage out of it for SRI).

So, have your policies right and decide on the right projects accordingly, rather than grab every single project.

See this example of a non-technical project: SRI had a prospective customer who was keen to procure their product. However, this came with 2 clauses. The prospective customer wanted SRI to supply it at a price that was lesser by 20 per cent than the price offered; the second clause was that the prospective customer wanted SRI to procure their organisation's tea and coffee requirements from his son, who was in the business of supplying tea and coffee. SRI was assured of good quality and discounted prices from his son. Should SRI accept the offer?

In order to arrive at the outcome, let us break it down into the following steps—and, most importantly, add the monetary impact to each step.

Step 1: Potential new business from prospective customer: Rs. 100,000

Step 2: Potential net margin on account of the above at reduced price: Rs.10,000.

Step 3: Potential saving from by procuring tea and coffee from the recommended source: Nil

Now you need to evaluate whether this new business, which is actually worth Rs. 10,000, is worthwhile for SRI to pursue or not. The final decision should be based on that.

Further break it down into pros and cons.

The following were the advantages SRI arrived at:

- Increases turnover, thereby helping move closer to the target.
- Increases margins by Rs. 10,000.
- Increased customer database.

Upon further analysis, SRI realised that:

- The quantum of business is miniscule and insignificant.
- If SRI supplies at the lower rates requested, it may lead to further drop of SRI's prices from existing customers.
- SRI does not want to spoil its relationship with your existing tea and coffee vendor.

What would you do if you were SRI?

If, after the above analysis, you feel that you should not accept the order, you can re-negotiate the price and then proceed if your offer is accepted. Or else, decline the offer, as it does not make much financial sense.

Now let us say in the above prospective that the client is a big brand and it is good to have such a customer as it adds value to your organisation. Then, your decision might be different.

So, look at all the factors and evaluate them objectively and holistically, and then assess them on a case-to-case basis. It is also very important for you to know and base your decisions on the financial impact. Of course, while financial impact will be a major factor, that alone cannot be the only deciding factor.

> Reflections:
> - *List down the advantages and disadvantages of the project under consideration.*
> - *What is the non-monetary impact that the project will have on your business?*
> - *What will be the long-term impact of the particular project?*

Product Profitability

> SRI's ventures were having many different products and business verticals. They wanted to evaluate the performance of each vertical in order to make prudent business decisions. Thus, SRI realised that they needed to calculate each individual product's profitability. How should they go about it? Are you aware?

If you are manufacturing, say, 5 different products or rendering various services for different verticals, it would be a financially healthy habit to compute the product profitability or the segmental profitability. It is important to undertake this exercise in order to know which product or segment gives you the maximum yield, to know the highest profit generator or, for that matter, to even know which customer contributes the most towards profitability.

Not only does it provide you clear visibility in terms of individual financial performance, it also helps you understand which areas you need to focus upon. It aids in planning ahead in terms of which product or service you need to sell more of in order to generate better profits or throws light on either increasing the selling price of a particular product or upscaling efforts in sales and so on, if a particular product is not selling as per your target.

To arrive at product profitability, you need to compute the difference between the revenue it generates and the total costs associated with the product or service over a specified period of time. The common costs and fixed costs can then be allocated to each product, based on pre-determined basis such as proportion of headcount or proportion of revenue or number of hours etc.

To illustrate, here is an example. SRI manufactures products A, B & C. In a particular month, 10 units of product A have been sold, 20 units of B and 30 units of C have been sold. The selling prices for each unit are Rs. 50,000, Rs. 30,000 and Rs. 20,000 respectively. The respective costs of production of each unit are Rs. 20,000, Rs. 10,000 and Rs. 12,000. The fixed costs include rent of Rs. 100,000 per month, general administrative costs of Rs. 340,000 per month and support salary costs of Rs. 200,000 per month. The floor space occupied for the production is in the ratio of 5:3:2. The number of employees working on production of A, B and C are 10, 6 and 4 respectively. SRI wants to compute the product profitability.

What the Finance

	A	B	C	Total
Units sold	10	20	30	
Selling price/unit	50,000	30,000	20,000	
Total revenue	5,00,000	6,00,000	6,00,000	17,00,000
Cost of production of each unit	20,000	10,000	12,000	
Profit per unit	30,000	20,000	8,000	
Total production costs	2,00,000	2,00,000	3,60,000	7,60,000
Rent (allocated based on area occupied)	50,000	30,000	20,000	1,00,000
General administrative overheads (allocated based on revenue)	1,00,000	1,20,000	1,20,000	3,40,000
Support staff salary (allocated based on head count)	1,00,000	60,000	40,000	2,00,000
Total costs	4,50,000	4,10,000	5,40,000	14,00,000
Profit	50,000	1,90,000	60,000	3,00,000

Note the following from the above:

1. Highest units sold – Product C
2. Highest selling price per unit – Product A
3. Highest profit per unit – Product A
4. Highest overall profit – Product B

So, which product should SRI focus on? Is it worthwhile to produce all 3 products?

Based on the above computation and market conditions, SRI can decide on the following:

- To sell more of Product B as that fetches the highest overall profit per unit.
- Or, depending on the scope for sale, SRI may decide not to focus as much on Product A as that generates the least overall profit.
- If SRI wants to focus on increasing the top line, SRI may want to focus on Product A.
- Since Product C is giving the least profit per unit, SRI may think of discontinuing it.

By weighing all pros and cons, you can decide as per your requirements. Your vital business decisions can be arrived at based on such analysis. Similar analysis can be done for each business vertical, to compute the vertical-wise profitability.

> **Reflections:**
> - *How will you arrive at the cost of your services for various verticals?*
> - *How will you allocate interest costs to each vertical?*
> - *What are the vertical specific costs for each of the respective verticals?*

5S

> While reading a book, Ram chanced upon the term 'Kaizen', which is a Japanese term for continuous improvement in all aspects of the organisation. Ram thought about how it could be used in SRI to better themselves. How would you like to improve your business further?

Kaizen can be a powerful tactic, which offers many benefits like waste elimination, improved productivity, improved quality, improved safety, lower costs, satisfied customers and so on. Further, Kaizen focuses on creative solutions instead of incurring capital expenditures.

One of the main tools of Kaizen is known as 5S. Each 'S' denotes a better and more efficient manner to do the routine.

- Sort – This implies the need to get rid of clutter. You need to remove all unnecessary items from your workplace.
- Set in order – Means organising the workplace. A place for everything and everything in its place. Create a specific location for everything.
- Shine – Have a shining and sparkling clean work area.
- Standardise – Standardise the best practice within your organisation.

Establish schedules, methods and processes for different activities.
- Sustain – Continue doing the above for sustained results. Get all your associates across levels to be involved to achieve sustained gains.

The results that are possible by implementing the above are improved profitability, higher efficiency, safety, better service and greater customer satisfaction.

For an entrepreneur to improve business performance the 5S can be:

- Solve – Problems or issues.
- Spend – Time, money and energy on your business.
- Sell – As much as you can.
- Surplus – Maximise the amount left after meeting all your expenses.
- Sustain – Your business to keep growing.

> **Reflections:**
> - *What else, apart from 5S, can you do towards further improvement within your organisation?*
> - *How do you think it will impact your results?*
> - *What are the steps required to be taken to implement them?*

Make or Buy

> One of the businesses of SRI's ventures was into manufacturing. There was a shortage in the market of one of the raw materials that was required for manufacturing, which affected their business. While they were pondering over how to tackle the issue, one of their board advisors asked if SRI had considered manufacturing the raw material. That was when SRI thought about this option of 'make versus buy'. Have you also faced such a dilemma?

This is one of the key dilemmas many manufacturing organisations face: Whether you have to manufacture in-house or purchase from suppliers. There are many factors that can help you determine the best bet for you.

Some of the factors that you may want to think about in your decision-making are:

- Financial impact in the short-term as well as long-term.
- Volumes required.
- Your level of expertise.
- Timelines to be met.
- Capacity utilisation.
- Human resource availability.
- Technological aspects.
- Availability when required.
- Quality and reliability of the product under introspection.
- Cost benefit analysis (after including other hidden charges/overheads in either option).
- Intellectual property rights.
- Economies of scale.

The above factors can also be used to evaluate the two options of undertaking a particular activity in-house or outsourcing it to a specialist (such as payroll services, housekeeping services and so on).

Products with low contributions can be bought (or outsourced) if the released capacity can be used to produce products with higher contribution. Options like forward integration (for business expansion to include distribution or supply of the products) or backward integration (purchase or merger with suppliers) can also be deliberated upon while evaluating 'make or buy' decisions.

> **Reflections:**
> - *What are the other factors, apart from the above, that you need to consider when choosing 'make or buy'?*
> - *Explore areas where you can buy instead of make. List the pros and cons.*
> - *What are the possibilities of having other alternatives instead of make or buy?*

Diversification

> During one stage of business, Sid, Ram and Isha were discussing the diversification of SRI. Each of the founders had a different thought about it and they were unable to decide on what the right thing was. Newer verticals, newer markets, newer geographies, newer products? They felt confused. So, they decided to ask their business coach, who asked them to list their purpose for diversification and whether it was in line with their overall objective. As soon as this exercise was completed, the trio were able to get some clarity on their thoughts on diversification and how to go about the same. What are your thoughts on diversification of your business? What is your purpose?

As the business grows, it is essential that the business expands (new products, new territories and so on) and you may also think of diversifying into new areas. While it is a good decision, you need to know when it is the right time to venture into this big decision of expansion or diversion.

During my interaction with some business owners, I understood that some of them burnt their fingers by taking this plunge too soon. You will have to carefully evaluate the right time to penetrate new territories or introduce new products/services. It should have the right balance between the financial perspective and the business perspective.

Financially, some of the parameters you can think of are:

- What is the amount of extra funds at your disposal?
- If you are opting for a loan or getting it funded, what is your capacity to repay/show the results to your investors?
- How will this new project be financially independent?
- How stable are you in the current business/territory?
- When you have not conquered in the existing market (or conquered with the existing product), how will you establish in the new terrain?
- What can be the worse-case scenario? How equipped are you for it?
- Are you biting off more than you can chew?

- Have you discussed this option with your mentor, high performance coach, business coach or someone who can help you in arriving at the right decision?

Note that the above list is not exhaustive—it is a guide to help you think things through on similar lines when you are pondering over such issues.

If you have satisfied yourself with your answers to the questions above (and other ones that you have thought through), you are probably in a position to move forward.

> **Reflections:**
> - *What is the due diligence/market research that you have carried out on the diversification that you are considering?*
> - *What is your capacity to bounce back if this expansion/diversity fails?*
> - *How will you know when is the right time to diversify and grow further?*

Creating Reserves

> SRI's profits of the past few years were partly distributed amongst the founders, and the remainder was reinvested into the business. At one point, there was severe market recession and business was dull. SRI did not have a fallback at that time and felt the distress. Their board advisor asked if they had any reserves as a cushion—only then did SRI learn it the hard way. Do you have sufficient reserves to back you up on a rainy day?

I would call your attention to Page 50 where we spoke about holding around one-third of earnings towards the reserves of your organisation. A reserve is nothing but profits that have been set aside for a predetermined purpose.

Reserves may be required, especially for contingencies, unforeseen events, business expansion, to wade through troubled times, investment opportunities, mergers and acquisitions and so on. This is known as general reserve. As the name suggests, this reserve is created without any specific or particular purpose.

Apart from this, specific reserves can also be created as per your requirements—for example, to pay for a long-drawn legal case, to procure certain assets, statutory reserves and so on.

The best way to continue to create general reserves would be up until a point when the business is well established, and by parking the excess funds into a separate reserve—importantly, ensuring that these funds are not withdrawn periodically. Whatever in your opinion is required to be set aside for any business contingencies or emergencies must be set aside, as that amount can be used at a future date either for further growth or any other issues as the case may be.

These funds, meant as general reserve (or as specific reserves), can be invested into liquids funds, fixed deposits or other interest generating avenues in order to optimise their utilisation.

> **Reflections:**
> - *What do you think can be the upside and downside of having reserves for your organisation?*
> - *How will you feel when you have sufficient resources as a backup?*
> - *What do you need to do to create reserves?*

Now that you are more equipped with the above pointers towards handling the financial performance of your business, there are a few other things that will take you to the next level in getting better with your business finance. The fact is that there is no end to getting things better. The best bet is to resort to the 'Kaizen' or constant improvement even in your business finance.

With this in mind, let us proceed to see what will take you further in managing the financial performance of your business even better.

Chapter 8

WHAT WILL TAKE YOU FURTHER

This section provides you with some generic tips that can contribute towards the healthier financial performance of your organisation. Hence, I am no longer using the example of SRI. Feel free to build around the points that will suit your requirements. You can customise these as per your needs and also come up with strategies similar to these, which will benefit the growth of your business and also help in better performance of not only your top line but also increased profits. Get the extra financial mileage!

Investor Returns

One of the prime reasons investors invest in your business is that they seek good returns on their investment. If you do not have an external investor, remember that you are the investor in your business. If your business were run efficiently, there would be good profits. After retaining some amount within the company (depending on the scope for further growth prospects, contingencies of the business and other requirements), the rest can be distributed as returns to your investors, thus giving them a reason to smile.

Here is a pictorial depiction of what will make your investors happy. As the business owner(s), you need to be always watchful of your organisations performance and financial status. Some areas for improving the operating performance of your company are:

- Innovation.
- Customer satisfaction.
- Excellence.

WHAT THE FINANCE

And some areas for improving the financial aspects of your company are:

- Internal controls.
- Cost controls.
- Efficiency.

The abbreviation for both the above are ICE, and so I am referring to them as 'eyes'!

Have an ear for the industry trends in order to be aware of the latest and also perceive any business risks that may be mitigated.

Just as you breathe constantly, you need to be constantly updated with technology developments, adopting effective strategy and lead on expertise. So, this forms the nose.

The above leads to increased productivity, increase in profits and thereby increasing the returns of your shareholders/investors, thus giving them a reason to smile. When you put these together as a picture, the below is what you get!

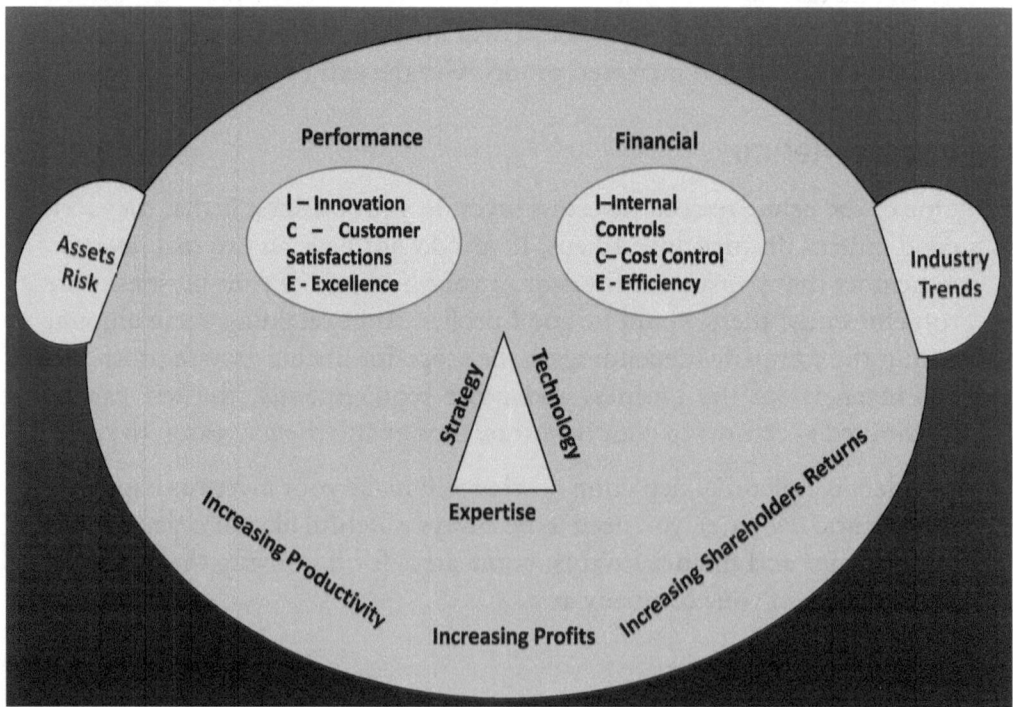

> **Reflections:**
> - *How will you feel when the returns from the business are high?*
> - *What are the other areas you need to focus on, to maximise returns?*
> - *What do you think are the gaps you need to fix to enhance returns?*

Financial Jaws

Financial jaws represent the growth of your revenue and margin over a period of time. If you are selling a product at Rs. 100 each, and the cost of each product is Rs. 90, it is obvious that you make a margin of Rs. 10 on each sale. Therefore, by the law of extrapolation, if you sell 1,000 units, your costs will be Rs. 90,000 and your margin will be at Rs. 10,000. Here, the profit grows purely by increase in volume.

However, in real life, we know it seldom happens this way. There may be healthy growth of the revenue but, along with the revenue, your costs are also growing. In such a case, the margins may decrease both as a percentage and also, sometimes, in absolute terms.

When we plot the revenue growth and compare it with the costs, the two lines are meant to represent the jaws. Therefore, in an ideal situation, the wider the jaw, the better the financial performance of your organisation. It means that, while the revenue increases, the costs decrease and, thereby, the profits are maximising. Hence, the wider the jaw, the better the financial status.

Look at the following information for better understanding:

Case 1:

Year	Sales in '000s	Cost in '000s	Profit in '000s	Profit %
1	1000	900	100	10%
2	1400	1230	170	12%
3	2000	1880	120	6%
4	2700	2520	180	7%
5	3200	3150	50	2%

When the above data is represented as a graph:

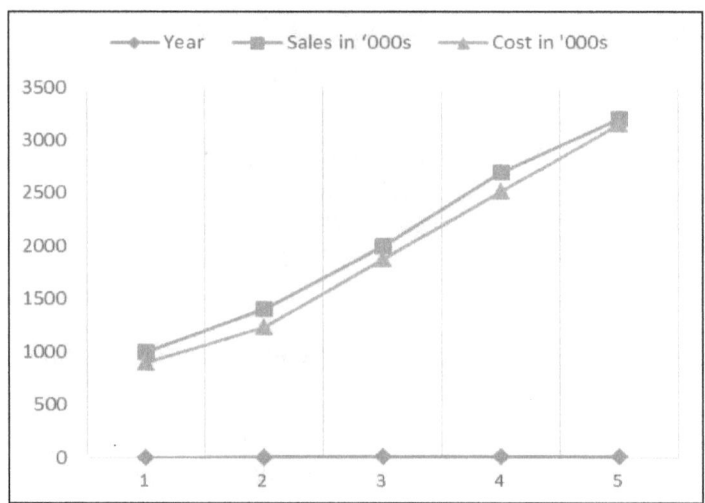

In this case, you will notice that while the revenue has grown year-on-year, the costs have also grown—thereby, profit has not grown as a percentage of the revenue. In fact, in year 3 and year 5, profits have dropped as absolute numbers as well.

In such situations, ask yourself if you want only the revenue to grow or if you also want the profits to grow and take necessary steps accordingly for the same.

Case 2:

Year	Sales in '000s	Cost in '000s	Profit in '000s	Profit %
1	1000	900	100	10%
2	1400	1200	200	14%
3	2000	1640	360	18%
4	2700	2250	450	17%
5	3200	2500	700	22%

When the above data is represented as a graph:

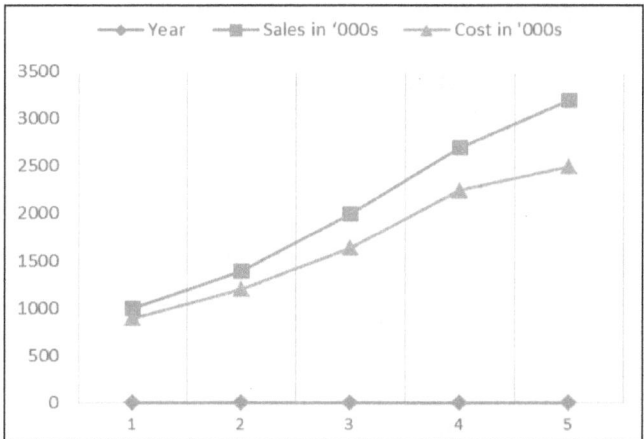

In this scenario, you will observe that, as the revenue has grown, the costs have been decreasing, thereby providing a wider jaw, implying that the profits are growing, too.

As the business owner, you need to strive to achieve this ideal scenario of increasing revenues and decreasing costs—thereby, the jaws getting wider, indicating maximising the profits of your business. So, you need to focus on widening the financial jaws.

There could be exceptions to the above rule of widening the jaws. For example, you know that you want to achieve a certain target of revenue, as it may be beneficial in the long term for your organisation. In cases like these, you take a conscious decision of revenue growth for which you may have to incur higher costs, thereby decreasing your profits but making good the case in future years.

> Reflections:
> - *What does your present financial jaws reveal about your business?*
> - *What actions do you need to take to widen the financial jaws of your business?*
> - *Project your financial jaws for the next 5 years to keep it as a yardstick for measuring your actual performance.*

Risk Mitigation

Irrespective of the nature of your business, risk of all sorts is a threat that hangs right above you. As a shrewd businessperson, you need to first be aware of the potential risks and then be sure to take necessary steps to mitigate the same.

In order to assess your risk, you need to first be aware of the risks that are concerning your business. Evaluate from all aspects. Some probable areas can be:

- How prepared are you should you lose your Man Friday?
- What will happen if your prime customer severs business relation with you?
- If your key vendor shuts shop, who is your next in line?
- Should your relationship with your investor or co-founder turn sour, what will you do?
- How will you handle expectation mismatch with your customer/supplier/employee and so on?
- To minimise foreign exchange risks, do you want to hedge?

These questions are intended to provide you with some different perspectives from which you can assess risks from different aspects. Of course, this list is not complete. It is just to provide you a flavour.

While all businesses thrive on their customers, check on some of these aspects of your organisation.

- Is over 80 per cent of your organisation's revenue being generated from a single customer?
- Are you overly dependent on that one customer that the performance of your business is directly related to the performance of your customer?
- What happens if, for whatever reason, your single dependent customer ceases to give you further orders? Or if that customer is bankrupt?
- Do you have an alternate plan should something go wrong?
- What steps have you taken for your further business development?

Similarly, check the following for your suppliers/vendors:

- Are the major components/requirements of your business being supported by only one major supplier?
- What will be your business impact if the supplier either decreases his quality or increases his prices?
- What happens if that supplier is unable to deliver to you on time or there is an unforeseen delay from the supplier? How will it affect your business?
- What if that supplier is out of business?
- What are the alternatives from where you source your requirements?

While, practically, it may be good to deal with just the main single customer or supplier, keep other options open so that your business does not suffer should there be an adversity that affects your important customer/supplier.

You should also evaluate industry risks, foreign exchange risks, market risks, financial risks, business risks and so on, that are applicable to your business.

By looking at risks from various angles, you need to create win-win strategies so that all the concerned parties get the best possible solution of any impending challenges.

> Reflections:
> - *What do you think are the biggest risks for your business?*
> - *What actions have you taken for data security, data back-up, and so on? What are your Disaster Recovery Plan (DRP) and Business Continuity Plan (BCP)?*
> - *How will you take calculated risks?*

Window Dressing

Window dressing, as the name suggests, is used to dress and create an artificial display and does not portray the right picture. It is usually resorted to with the intent to misguide, create a false impression and paint a rosy picture.

At times, financial statements are window dressed to present a good performance to the shareholders, boost the share price when they are seeking new investment, secure new clients, to meet the year-end targets and so on. Financial results are manipulated to project favourable results.

From a legal perspective, window dressing can be considered fraudulent if it is not compliant with the laws and the accounting standards. The well-known examples are of Satyam Software and Enron, among others. Extra care and precaution needs to be adopted before any sort of window dressing.

A common example of window dressing is when sales personnel inflate the year-end sale to meet their internal target and reverse the sale at the beginning of next year, thereby ensuring they obtain their sales bonus for the current year. Be watchful of such traps.

As the business owner, you can build the right culture in your organisation and lead by example, so as to not get into the culture of window dressing.

> Reflections:
> - *How will window dressing impact your business?*
> - *What will be the impression your brand will create when it is known that your books have been window dressed?*
> - *How will you feel about window-dressed financials?*

Ethics

I cannot stress more on the importance of ethics, integrity and transparency, especially with your customers as this will go a long way in taking your relationship to the next level and over the long term. Trust and respect are built on the foundation of ethics that you and your team carry and represent. Ethics becomes one of the core values that your organisation will be known for. Further, this is also the message you are indirectly giving your staff, who are expected to follow suit.

By being transparent with your customer, you are being truthful. For example, if there are hidden costs/extra costs that will be incurred by the customer, be upfront about it, rather than giving them a rude shock at a later date. This will also enable your customer to plan his budget accordingly. This will also help you build your credibility in business.

Similarly, refrain from using materials of inferior quality just to increase your profits. Such a case may help you win temporarily but the damage to your name and brand will be permanent. It is better to be known for the quality of your product, which will eventually get you more business—and, thereby, your profits will automatically increase in the long run. Do not opt for short cuts. They may seem tempting but having your larger objective in mind will help you with the right decision on the right path. Dell Computers had to pay a fine of over $100 million in 2010 as it misled investors through false accounting to meet Wall Street expectations.

To give another example, if your customer wants the project to be completed by a certain date and you know it is not feasible, be open about it and commit to a realistic timeframe rather than trying to keep the customer happy momentarily.

It is always wiser to under-commit and over-deliver as that will help you exceed your customers' expectations.

> Reflections:
> - *What sort of ethics culture are you building in your organisation?*
> - *What action will you take if you discover that your key personnel did not act ethically?*
> - *How will you pass on the importance of ethics to your team?*

Human Capital

When I visited Glasgow in Scotland, I noticed huge banners all over the city, which said, "People make Glasgow." I found it to be so true—and also realised that your people are the ones who make your organisation. If you have efficient employees, your organisation becomes a highly effective one.

The vice versa is also true. I cannot insist on how important the human capital of your organisation is. Your employees are your greatest strength.

Undoubtedly, your employees will give their very best when they are highly motivated and you as their employer can try and ensure that their enthusiasm and motivational levels are high and create a win-win strategy.

Small gestures of appreciation and rewarding the right employees will go a long way. For example, if an employee has come up with an innovative idea, reward him. You can do the same for new business generation or if the employee has contributed to improving the quality or productivity of the business. Ensure that there are no ego clashes between the teams, as you definitely do not want your star employee leaving your organisation at a crucial time. Hence, it is also a good idea to have a second-in-command or an alternative to a particular key employee, so that your routine operations are not affected. It would be good to have a succession plan in place.

Other measures, like sharing a part of the profits when the organisation has done very well in a particular year, boosts the morale of your employees and they will be willing to stretch themselves more—thereby contributing to the growth of your organisation.

> **Reflections:**
> - *How can you inculcate a growth mindset within your team?*
> - *How will you feel when you have a team of dedicated and trustworthy employees?*
> - *What can you do to form such a team?*

Understanding the Market

It is essential to understand the market trends, customer requirements, industry developments, competitors pitch and so on, in order to have a better edge on your offerings of service or manufacturing of your product. You can try to understand these by analysing consumer behaviours, conducting market surveys, online polls, or market research, which will provide you with a deeper outlook of the market and help you to grow.

Identifying the market gap or by being the first or the leader in your domain will fetch you larger financial gains and aid you in multiplying your profits. Studying consumer trends can be a good step towards revealing potential demand. If required, you can seek help of a market research firm for this purpose. Your marketing strategy should be customer-centric. Remember that customers' choices are driven based on the value offered, what they experience (with your product or service) and the level of satisfaction derived.

By dividing the market into segments of customers, you can cater to your segments as per your strategic target customers. It is also essential to manage your existing customers, seek new customers and manage demand.

Financially, if it is a burden to resort for heavy marketing expenses—it may be a good alternative to resort to digital marketing or guerrilla marketing techniques.

Customer relationship management is the overall process of building and maintaining profitable customer relationships by delivering superior value and satisfaction. Customer satisfaction is the extent to which a product's (or service's) perceived performance matches a buyer's expectations.

It is also essential to build the right relationships with the right customers. It involves treating your customers as assets that need to be managed and maximised. Hence, build the right relationship with the right customers. Obtaining feedback from customers is a great means to ensure you are catering to as well as serving your customers in the right manner.

Further, explore options of upselling or cross-selling with your customers. Upselling refers to the practice of selling a comparable high-end product to your customers; cross-selling refers to selling of related or complimentary items to your customers. By resorting to these, you stand to increase your top line and, eventually, your profits.

> **Reflections:**
> - *Which are the markets you think have the scope for further penetration?*

> - *What else can be done to get a better understanding of the market, the market trends, customer requirements and so on? How will you get to know the emerging trends of your industry?*
> - *What will give you a clear picture of the market potential?*

Mitigation of Losses

Profits (and losses) tend to fluctuate between periods. You need to look for ways and means to overcome the losses. If the losses are recurring in nature, you need to decipher the best way to come out of the loss and convert it into a turnaround to profit. Check profit or loss of each activity.

Some indicators that can help you for the turnaround:

- Are you over-spending?
- How are you preventing the losses? What steps have you taken in this regard?
- Is your product/service catering to the requirements of the customers?
- How are you sourcing your clients?
- Are you investing enough in business development?
- Summarise the lessons you have learnt from your mistakes in the past.
- What other alternatives can you consider to grow your business?
- Invest in a mentor/coach/industry expert who can guide you.
- Draft the way forward.
- Perform a SWOT analysis of your business and seek ways to work on the areas for improvement.
- Lay out a system for better cash flow management.
- Be the first, be the leader or be unique or offer differentiation in your product or service.
- Remember, magic happens outside your comfort zone.
- Take calculated risks and mitigate the risks that are not under your control.

> **Reflections:**
> - *What can you do differently from the past, which will result in mitigation of losses?*
> - *What is the turnaround time that you are considering?*
> - *Whom can you talk to or consult, regarding mitigating your losses?*

Other Parameters for Measurement

As an entrepreneur, you need to assess a few other parameters to measure the progress of your business. This may vary from industry to industry and organisation to organisation. However, to give you an idea of the kinds of parameters to be watchful of, here are some pointers. You can customise them as per your requirements. You can dissect these parameters as you want, depending on what you seek. This will give you a different perspective to your business approach.

Here is the sample:

- Cost per employee.
- Revenue generated per employee.
- Profit per employee.
- Attrition rate.
- Capital investment per employee.
- Overheads cost per employee.
- Net profit per product/service.
- Profit generated by each department or vertical.
- Total cost of each department.
- Percentage of each cost item as against the revenue.
- Region-wise revenue/cost.
- Profit for each product/line of service.
- Return on investment for each vertical.
- Education and experience mix of employees.

You can further compare these numbers with the industry standards to gauge your performance. Also, you can interpret these parameters in such a manner as to focus growth on respective areas as desired.

> **Reflections:**
> - *What are the other parameters you would like to consider?*
> - *How does it reflect on the financial health of the organisation?*
> - *How often would you want to monitor these parameters?*

Redesigning Processes

For maximising your profits, evaluate other means where you can redesign processes that will help in minimising your costs/time involved. As an entrepreneur, you will know the best. However, I am suggesting a few ideas that will help kindle your thought process for your business. Feel free to mull over such ideas/thoughts to see if any of these can be implemented or if any of these can be modified further to suit your requirements.

- Re-structuring workflows.
- Processes that can be eliminated.
- Cutting out unwanted steps.
- Automation of processes.
- Simplification of steps.
- Re-engineering workspaces.
- Eliminating processes that do not add value to the customer.
- Adopting a unique marketing strategy.
- Ways to get lead generation.
- Different ways to convert leads into customers.
- Reducing machine downtime.
- Offering a better customer experience.
- Efficient use of technology.
- Higher efficiency through innovative processes.
- Better waste management procedures in place.

- Improving organisational efficiency through lean methodology and six sigma.
- Ways to increase your customer base.

The above list is only an indicative one. Please build further on these lines to suit your business needs.

> **Reflections:**
> - *With your standard process routines, what can you do differently that will result in a beneficial process?*
> - *What would make you attempt different process and think out of the ordinary?*
> - *How can you simplify the existing processes?*

Waste Management

The waste generated by your organisation can arise either directly or indirectly. Whichever way it is, by managing waste better, you can reduce your costs and thereby increase your potential savings. Direct waste is primarily derived from manufacturing organisations due to the result of the manufacturing activity. On the other hand, indirect waste can assume many other forms and can arise on account of various activities (such as water waste, food waste, paper waste, electricity waste and so on)

Direct waste, if managed better, can lead to better savings as it has a financial impact. Waste arising directly from manufacturing activity is popularly known as 'The seven wastes of lean manufacturing'. The acronym to remember here is 'TIMWOOD'. Let us take a quick look at each of them as below:

- T stands for transportation. This arises from movement of the product between processes. Transporting your product or parts of your product from one place to another does not add any further value to your product and is hence considered to be a waste of both time and energy. Hence, by keeping transportation to a minimum, you can produce more efficiently. To effect this, you can evaluate having processes near each other, keeping the pathways clear ands so on.

- I for inventory. Raw materials, work in progress and finished goods constitute inventory. Inventory consumes your space and costs you money. Inventory waste arises on account of excess produced. One of the ways for lean manufacturing is known as 'Just in Time' or producing only when required by customers. You can further reduce the changeover time, work in smaller batches, adhere to laid out procedures and so on.
- M denotes motion. This includes all sorts of motion—such as movement of people or machines, thus creating waste of time and energy like searching for tools, climbing, bending, lifting and so on, which causes fatigue and depletes energy. Thus, by proper planning, better workstation layout, redesigning and so on, you can reduce stress and delay, thus minimising motion waste.
- W indicates waiting, which creates idle time. Waiting can be of men, material, machine product or information—and this causes inefficiency. Waiting can be due to process delay, unreliable people or machines, delayed inputs and so on. By eliminating the waiting time, you can utilise the time towards better productivity.
- O is for over-production. When you produce more than required or produce before it is required, it is said to be over production. The excess produced needs storage, transportation and has a financial impact, which is a waste that could be avoided. You can overcome this by producing smaller batches, having reliable processes, and utilising accurate forecasts.
- O stands for over-processing. Over-processing (for example, creating multiple inspections, redundant documentation, multiple counting or checking and so on) consumes more time and effort than required and is considered a waste. This can be avoided by standardising techniques, setting clear expectations and sound quality controls in place.
- D refers to defects. It requires extra effort, rework cost and so on. Defects affect the entire output. You need to lower the frequency of defects by improving processes, provide sufficient training, reduce operational errors and so on.

Some of the common waste minimisation techniques are:
- Avoid.
- Reduce.

- Reuse.
- Recycle.
- Recover.
- Treat.
- Dispose responsibly.

Although the concept of TIMWOOD is mainly for manufacturing organisations, some of the areas can also be implemented by the non-manufacturing organisations to minimise waste.

> Reflections:
> - *Where is your time and energy being wasted currently?*
> - *How can you prioritise the important ones and eliminate the waste from your routine?*
> - *What will you gain by minimising the waste?*

General Tips

Here are some very generic tips that can contribute towards improving your organisation's margins:

- Understand and calculate the financial implication of your business decisions.
- Have the second line in command for each major department especially in cases of emergencies.
- Your employees are your biggest assets. Remember, they are not human resources but human capital.
- Build your business on a scalable basis.
- To flourish more, your product or service should resolve problems/challenges faced; else, there should be a good demand for it.
- Develop blue ocean strategies for your business.
- Think big. Will 2 big deals be better than say 10 smaller deals?
- Have you evaluated a franchising model of your business? Alternatively, other direct selling business models like Tupperware, Amway, or Herbalife can be looked into.

- While computing your costs, remember to include the cost of carrying inventory and other such related costs.
- Is there anything you can do differently in the existing processes? Any unwanted/time-consuming processes that can be eliminated or combined or rearranged or replaced? What are the other alternatives that can be explored? Is there a way to simplify the process?
- Your readiness and level of gearing up to embrace the VUCA (Volatile, Uncertain, Complex, Ambiguous) world.

> **Reflections:**
> - *What are the other sources from where you can get to know about entrepreneurial tips?*
> - *Anyone who can help you in the process of guiding you, mentoring you or coaching you regarding your business?*
> - *What will make you think differently about your business processes and business deals?*

Common Mistakes to Watch Out For

Listed below are some common traps young entrepreneurs fall into. I am summarising them for easy reference.

- Filing of yearly income tax returns for your organisation (even if you are making a loss) within due dates.
- Fixed assets need to be depreciated.
- Need to differentiate between cash profits and book profits.
- The profit from one business vertical being eaten up due to loss from another business vertical.
- If you are asset rich and cash poor, your liquidity is impacted.
- Apply applicable TDS rates on your payments.
- Differentiate between a year (can be financial year or calendar year) and a period (can be a period of say 3 months or 6 months or even let's say 18 months).
- Applying correct tax rates.

> **Reflections:**
> - *What are the other ways of maximising your profits?*
> - *How can you grow your network?*
> - *What do you think are the traps you need to be watchful of?*

Avenues To Learn More About Finance

If you are keen to learn more about finance with regard to your business, you can try to supplement with any or all of the following options:

- Online courses.
- Attending seminars like 'Finance for Non-finance'.
- Reading more books on finance.
- Having a finance mentor.
- Talking to industry experts.
- Having in-depth conversation with your finance consultant/auditor.
- Networking with your contacts who are familiar with such topics and seeking their opinion.
- Hiring a business coach or high performance coach.

> **Reflections:**
> - *What are the benefits you will get by learning more about finance?*
> - *How can you sustain your interest in financial management?*
> - *How will you feel when you have a good grip on the finances of your business?*

With this, the crux of the book is complete. However, I am not stopping here, as I would like you to be engaged further with some real-life inspirational stories of entrepreneurs and their learning. I hope you enjoy and cherish their journey as much as I enjoyed interacting with them.

Chapter 9

WHAT IS YOUR INSPIRATION

In this section, I am sharing the financial journeys, perspectives, views, learning and challenges of some successful and well-known entrepreneurs.

I further wish that you gain inspiration from their stories and work around their words of wisdom. Pick your role models and get inspired to fly high!

Polarity Management—Dilemmas of an Entrepreneur

(Arun Jain, Founder & Former Chairman, Polaris Consulting & Services Ltd.; Chairman & Managing Director Intellect Design Arena Ltd., Chennai, India)

The engineer from a large family in Delhi wanted to live only in India. He learnt at a young age about bad debts, the consequences of not protecting intellectual property, the fact that the software industry banks on intellectual capital and that only a minimum financial capital was required. In 1983, along with two other friends, he started a partnership firm called International Information Systems, which was later converted into a private limited company called Nucleus that sold software products. Four years later, a project with his client, Citibank, brought him to Chennai, a place that is now his home. As the founders of Nucleus were spread across different geographies, for easier decision-making, they started three different companies—thus was born Polaris, which was headed by Arun Jain (AJ). He shares his views on how an entrepreneur has to learn to 'thrive' in the vulnerable zone.

The Pricing Dilemma

From his vast years of experience, AJ shares some of his distinct thoughts on arriving at the right pricing:

- As an entrepreneur, he insists that it is important to have clarity about the purpose of your business.
- You need to be aware of what is the customer's problem that you, as an entrepreneur, are solving. He further asks you to introspect on what is the problem that you are solving, which no one else has solved till now.
- If you do not have proper clarity on what you are solving, you are unaware of the value you are creating, thus resulting in a pricing that is probably incorrect.
- The right pricing and revenue model should revolve around the intensity of the pain that you are solving for your customer.
- Your solution is to aim to solve the highest pain of the customer, which will enable you to charge a premium price as well.
- If you do not choose your problem statement correctly, it could pose a challenge in your pricing.

The Funding Dilemma

Further, AJ has unique views with regard to funding. Unlike the earlier days, when businesses were mostly bootstrapped, there are currently many avenues to obtain funding. However, in his view, the mistake investors tend to make is to seek a business plan from the founders. He says he fails to understand how a start-up can provide a forward-looking P&L statement when he is unsure of the pricing at the start. He strongly feels that seeking a business plan is counter-intuitive to entrepreneurship. Only stable businesses can have business plans and not a start-up, in his perspective. As venture capitalists (VC) are not entrepreneurs themselves, they fail to understand this aspect, he feels. He is not all for VCs seeking ROI from start-ups initially; if they are keen on ROI, they need to invest in listed companies or regular business, he advises. Therefore, he feels VCs need to invest in a business depending on the capability of problem-solving as well as the commitment level of the team of the founders.

The Juggling Dilemma

AJ talks of the 6 different kinds of capital that are important to a business. He equates the capital to a ball. The 6 balls an entrepreneur has to learn to work on and juggle with are:

1. Brand: Although Polaris was a relatively small company at the time it started, it succeeded in creating the brand 'Polaris'. This brand awareness was created from the initial stages, like painting the transport buses, which were plying all over the city, with 'Polaris'. Further, in the arterial road of Chennai, Polaris sponsored the traffic lights in return for the name 'Polaris' to be featured at the busy traffic light junction. Despite low investment, multiple ways to create the brand awareness were incorporated. He emphasises that branding is not to be confused with the product marketing.

2. End customer: He/she becomes the sales person as well as the brand ambassador. The customer, by word of mouth, refers you to others, thus enabling growth of your business. Apps like WhatsApp, despite not having salespersons employed, have grown through word of mouth alone, thereby making customer capital very powerful.

3. Leadership: A single person cannot handle all the 6 balls; it is essential to have a strong team. Hence, partnership is important. Expertise is required in all the areas as they are intertwined. It is essential to hire the right people who can lead the team.

4. Intellectual Property: Product capital contributes to about 20 per cent of the entrepreneurship. The remaining 80 per cent form the other 5 types of capital. This capital exists with all business and the key is to sharpen the problem that is being solved. Designing and messaging are crucial and requires to be well articulated. The benefit of the product needs to be communicated to the customer as briefly as possible, else the retention is lost.

5. Execution: Revolves around excellence in delivery. It is important to deliver as promised and within the timeframe committed to the customer.

6. Finance: While the first 5 are intangible and not measurable, finance capital is measurable. The finance capital is strengthened

by the performance of the other 5 capital. Once clarity exists on the other 5 capital, financially the business will succeed AJ claims.

Thus, AJ insists that a VC should consider all the above aspects before deciding to invest.

The Dilemma of Parting with Equity

Multiple sources are available to raise capital. An entrepreneur should be concerned about how quickly the capital is required at each stage of the business life cycle, until which time the entrepreneur needs to be patient and manage within a shoestring budget, especially until the product is validated and the initial few customers are obtained. The next stage is testing the product and discovering the value, which usually takes 2 to 3 years. Thus, within the initial 3 years, it is not right to expect returns—else, it will lead to frustration and anxiety.

A dilemma in parting with the equity stake requires a mindset shift, he claims. There are newer ways in the market that ought to be explored, such as:

- One of the options could be, instead of the conventional parting with a fixed percentage of equity, during the first round of raising fresh capital, the angel investors are offered a stake through capital discounting by minimum baseline valuation and dividing capital into multiple stages based on various valuation metrics.
- Crowd funding can be yet another option to raise further capital.
- When the funding requirement is high and the investor is willing to take a higher risk based on trust factor and is blindly investing, a part of the investment could be offered as equity, based on the industry benchmark, as idea capital.

One of the financial dilemmas that he faced was whether to dilute the stake with private equity investors or not. While he had the choice to remain happy with the existing level of turnover in the mid-1990s, AJ was thinking big and realised that he required private equity to grow further, to acquire his own building and so on, and he is extremely happy with this decision, which was taken decades ago.

The Dilemma of Conscious vs. Subconscious Planning

AJ is a visionary, a strong team player as well as a believer in the power of subconscious goals. He recollects how his team, in the year 1993, visualised that, within 7 years, the turnover of the company would grow from Rs. 2 crore per annum to Rs. 100 crores. The secret, he says, is in not dividing this mammoth growth annually, as it would make the team feel jittery. By not doing so, in reality, they achieved over a hundred times growth within the 7-year horizon, which AJ credits more to the power of common subconscious planning than conscious planning. Fear limits the strategic thinking and hence growth of more than 20 to 30 per cent is usually considered a herculean task to achieve. Yet, growth can be multi-fold if the purpose is clear and the universe conspires as well.

The Dilemma of 'Letting Go'

Businesses should aspire to move onto the next orbit instead of rotating in the same orbit, he claims. For shifting the orbit, extra energy and extra risk appetite are required, which is what he has learnt from the many years of experience.

He asserts that, from Polaris, they have moved to Intellect—a new orbit—thus making them vulnerable, which was also a key learning for AJ and team. He prefers to choose vulnerability and move out from the comfort zone, as it is a place of learning and for creating exponential shifts.

AJ's mantra for risk mitigation is that he questions himself on what could be the worst outcome for any given situation, thus reducing the fear quotient. This is what drove him to invest Rs. 500 crore on creating and marketing the global brand of Intellect. Define the *minimum viable limits* before taking the plunge, he advises.

Technology kills itself with the introduction of Artificial Intelligence, robots and so on, thus driving him to segregate the services business from product business, as their DNA is different from each other, he explains. Forecasting that the technology life cycle is usually around 30 to 40 years. Gauging that the operating leverage of the services business was reducing, AJ felt it was the best to sell his bigger brand of Polaris. He further felt that pricing, arbitrage and technology alone could not be leveraged upon thus making a conscious choice to sell Polaris.

As parting words of wisdom, he states that an entrepreneur should also master the art of letting go and know that size does not matter. That is why he demerged and let go of the bigger (services) business of Polaris and retained the smaller (product) business of Intellect with the aim that the smaller business needs to grow bigger. With the aggressive growth plans in the global market, Intellect is ready to rule the industry.

***

Dare To Care

(Dr Arokiaswamy Velumani, Founder, Chairman & Managing Director, Thyrocare Technologies Ltd., Mumbai, India)

Being born in a village to poor parents, sleeping in the Bombay railway station at the start of his career and then becoming one of the richest Indians is no mean feat. With a high appetite for risk and wanting to enjoy the joy ride of thrills that life offers is this entrepreneur, who opts to dare at every stage in his life. Despite running Thyrocare successfully since 1996, Arokiaswamy Velumani (AV) does not own a house, does not travel in business class and believes in living a frugal lifestyle. He says his initial poverty made him powerful as it has helped him realise the value of money.

Money Cannot Make Money

Contrary to the popular belief that one can make money using money, AV believes only stamina can make money. He points out the paradox that both money and stamina usually cannot co-exist.

Having studied in a government school, and with a college education from an economical institute, AV says that while education from a branded school is expensive, education as such is not costly. Which school you study in is not as important as how well you study, he claims. Lakhs of money are not required for great education, he emphasises, and quotes his own example of how he spent only Rs. 1,000 for his graduation and only Rs. 10,000 for his PhD qualification. Being the oldest of three siblings, he shouldered the family responsibility and, right from his childhood, adapted himself to manage finances wisely—and learnt that one does not require money to make money.

Financial Prudence

Growing up in a not-so-well-to-do family and having conducted seven weddings for his family members, AV says he has learnt to use finance in a very prudent manner. Despite the fact that he was a government officer and his wife was a bank manager, they decided against buying a house, as they realised that they did not want to live beyond their means. This saved them the hassle of monthly loan repayment. He asserts how the current generation of people feel tied to their jobs and are unable to experience freedom of decision-making, only due to the pressure of repayment of their EMI. Due to his frugal attitude, he says that any unnecessary expenditure, even now, gives him sleepless nights.

Huge Capital Not Required To Get Started

Having worked for 14 years as a government officer for Bhabha Atomic Research Centre (BARC), AV decided to become his own boss. He set aside his savings bank balance of Rs. 2 lakhs for his family requirements, and had the comfort that his wife was continuing to work. The amount he received from his provident fund, which was another Rs. 2 lakhs, became the capital for Thyrocare.

AV shuns the myth that a huge amount of capital is required to start a business—unless, of course, the entrepreneur wants to drive fancy cars! He adds that only after the business started earning did he even buy the required office furniture. He wants the present-day youth to understand that money is required only to show off and not for starting a business.

Money Cannot Solve All Problems

AV defies the views of some people that, by opting for equity dilution and getting more money, all business problems can be solved. He urges people to focus on creating better teams and better people rather than seeking more funding. Even on building teams, he feels if you are looking for top-notch talent, it is expensive; freshers are not as expensive and are trainable as per requirement. Further, based on his past experience, he decided many years ago that he would recruit freshers for his organisation, thereby also providing them with opportunities.

He jokingly says, "No one opens the syringe before the customer opens his purse." By following this mantra, he has never really found the need to seek funding. Thus, his company has never borrowed and is debt free. He says, beaming, that Thyrocare is a cash-rich company as he is averse to borrowing.

Furthermore, borrowing money has its own set of challenges such as interest cost, which becomes a burden to repay, thereby weakening the business process, resulting in lack of efficiency and post-peak pains.

If at all you have to borrow, AV says:

- Borrow only when you can grow an established business, not for establishing a business.
- As a guideline, do not borrow more than 10 times your current profit.
- Borrowing and scaling up is essential if the business is capex-intensive.

Create Companies to Run Forever

If the focus of an entrepreneur is on market cap or valuation, AV feels the running of the company for a longer period diminishes. His business model is built around low capex and high opex. He has grown the company by building on volumes and has leveraged on it. He claims that an entrepreneur can either make money from the customer or the vendor—not both. Based on his growth, he negotiated with his vendors and gets a discount each time the volume grows. Thus, he based his business model on providing low rates to his customers and higher discounts from his vendors.

Yet another quote: "If you know the cost of goods sold (COGS) of your business, you can do business. But if you know the COGS of COGS, you can disrupt."

According to him, the power of his journey for the last two decades lies in not having withdrawn any money from the business, including his salary.

No company ever was closed down because of charging less, says AV. All failed companies could not control costs, in spite of charging more. His philosophy is to charge low, build volumes and enhance profits.

Leveraging on Credit for Better Cash Management

AV shares that his business model is driven on the power of cash credit with both his customers and suppliers. He illustrates this with an example. If an item can be sold at Rs. X and if you want to sell it at Rs.1.5 X, then credit needs to be extended. However, if it is sold at 0.75 X, the customer needs to pay in advance. Hence, he always receives money upfront from his customers.

Similarly, while negotiating with vendors, he offers to pay upfront, provided he can get more discounts. Thus, he manages both his cash inflow and outflow.

He cautions that some people collapse after seeing a huge amount simply because they become a victim of money; "Honey and money sound similar; if honeybee falls in honey, it dies and so does a moneybee!"

Expenditure vs. Investment

It is important to differentiate between expenditure and investment, insists AV. He regales how he had prolonged the decision to buy a car for Rs. 18 lakhs for his family whereas he bought medical equipment costing Rs.18 crores for his business in a single day. To him, the car was expenditure whereas the equipment was an investment. Learn to differentiate, he advises.

Valuation

Although he did not require it, he opted for private equity for the thrill of it. AV's views on private equity: "If you go to them, your value is 60 per cent, but if they come to you, your value is 160 per cent."

Again, for the sake of romancing with risk, he decided to take his company public. He is very glad about this decision of getting Thyrocare listed, as it has given him an identity and an iconic status.

Although the initial public offering (IPO) has a lot of costs, pains and challenges associated with it, it is worthwhile according to AV. If you have been running a transparent business, you would enjoy the outcome of the IPO, and its long-run advantages are worth it.

Risk Taking

AV, with a huge appetite for risk, claims that his rewards are high due to his ability to take calculated risks. He talks of two kinds of risk. The first where the upside is too good and the downside is too little. The second kind of risk is where the upside is little and the downside is too much. The first kind of risk is good to take but not the second kind, educates AV.

He further says that if you over-estimate risk, you will lose in life; if you underestimate risk, you will burn in life. As an entrepreneur, it is important that you need to have the ability to assess risk correctly.

Learnings

From his journey of 23 years, AV shares his message for the next generation of entrepreneurs.

- Create more. Consume less.
- Be a job creator. Skill and train your resources adequately. Keep redundant resources for growth since money cannot be made without people.
- With more stamina, you can make more money.
- Live like a crow (and share your knowledge), not like a dog (keeping it to yourself).
- Use money sensibly.

AV concludes by saying that the age of an entrepreneur and success as an entrepreneur are directly proportional, as higher the age, higher are the chances of success. The exception to this is when there is an innovation or a breakthrough. He substantiates his views by saying that to know the many aspects of business, like product, customer, market, HR, marketing, Finance, branding, logistics and so on takes time, which comes with age. When asked about his future plans, AV says without batting an eyelid he wants his company to go on forever.

***

Exit Info

(Badri Seshadri, Co-Founder & Former Director, Cricinfo.com, United Kingdom)

Many entrepreneurs dream of an exit that repays them multi-fold for all the efforts they had undertaken in building and operating a successful organisation. Does a Flipkart–Walmart sort of a deal happen in all exits? Does the founder make tons of money in all exits? Hear about it from Badri Seshadri (BS), as he shares his exciting journey with cricinfo.com, which he had started in 1996 and which was eventually acquired by ESPN in 2005.

Financial Education Is A Must

BS (who is currently the Managing Director of his second venture, New Horizon Media Pvt. Ltd.) insists on the importance of getting the finance principles right, right from the beginning. According to him, the common financial challenges that entrepreneurs face initially are:

- Not prioritising finance matters.
- Not having enough money while starting the business.
- Pondering about the sources of funding.
- Thinking of becoming profitable.
- Under-projection of the costs and unpredictable revenues.
- Not having sufficient financial skills to manage the business.

He asserts that entrepreneurs have to have the basic finance indicators intact and get a better understanding of financial management. Hence, he insists on a solid financial education for entrepreneurs so that they can manage the P&L, cash flow and projections, which are fundamental to running any successful business.

Financial Learning

He shares some of his financial learning from the time he started Cricinfo. He was unaware that an entrepreneur needs to know few basics related to finance and hence urges entrepreneurs to question themselves on some of these areas:

- When will your revenues exceed the costs?
- How many customers do you require to become profitable?
- How can you delay incurring some of the costs?
- Do you have the money to spend now?
- How will you make your ends meet?
- When to hire the right finance professional who can plug the holes at the right places?

He emphasises that entrepreneurs should have the ability to read numbers and that, during the initial phases, it is the job of the CEO to administer the finance function and not that of the bookkeeping accountant. While luck does favour a few entrepreneurs despite their lack of financial knowledge, he warns not to rely on luck alone, as there are still many areas, which require financial prudence. 'Build, Sell, Run' is not a business model that will work always he cautions.

Financial Gaffes

Claiming that Cricinfo is an example of a badly managed company in terms of finance, he credits its success to the dot.com boom of the 1990s. It started as a voluntary entity in 1993 with zero investment and then registered as a company in the United Kingdom in 1996. Until 1999, they still did not have much fund requirement but the scenario changed thereafter when they raised a lot of money—again, due to the dot.com boom.

Cricinfo obtained the initial seed money of GBP 100,000 due to their credible website and strong audience base despite having no revenues, no proper revenue model nor a business plan. To their surprise, yet another individual rich investor from the sports television background, who realised the potential of Cricinfo, was interested in their line of business and repaid the seed money and invested 30 times more in Cricinfo in return for a 25 per cent stake with the first (optional) right to exit. They built offices from the funding, as the investor was willing to take a chance with this business, despite no revenue. Luckily, their investor had hired capable financial consultant, who could foresee that they would soon run out of cash due to their expansion and so wanted to get a stable financial deal to encash on the 25 per cent stake.

In 1999, recalls BS, neither the top line nor the profitability of the ventures mattered to the investors. The metrics that the investors considered were the number of page views, unique users and so on as these could be monetised. Noticing that Cricinfo was looking at potential investors, BS was contacted by investment bankers, who created a solid business pitch for Cricinfo, in turn for a 2 per cent fee of the proceeds. A constructive business plan was documented by the investment bankers along with projections, audience base, reports from experts, scalability and so on, which paved the way for attracting investors. Offers started pouring in and they chose the best valuation, which was at US$150 million. Thus, in about a year, the initial investor was paid $20 million in the form of ADR (American Depository Receipts) and he more than quadrupled his investment out of his exit from Cricinfo by selling his stake, while BS and team decided to continue with the 75 per cent stake, given ADRs of $17.5 million and given additional shares in the process.

Yet another mistake that BS and team committed was not encashing the ADRs immediately when the stock prices rose by 10 to 15 per cent, where they could have invested in safe instruments. Two months thereafter, the stock market crashed and they lost huge amounts.

Despite having a huge bank balance obtained from the new investor, BS regrets that Cricinfo neither managed the amount nor built revenue streams. To top it, their monthly burn rate was at $1 million. They further hired an expensive sales team, but that did not result in an increase of revenues. There was still no business plan and they were mentally unclear where they were headed. It was partly because the investment bankers had promised them that the next round could be valued at around $250 million, due to the dot.com euphoria.

However, the environment changed within a year. The investment banker backed out as the dot.com crashed and the valuation of Cricinfo nosedived to only about GBP 5 million as against their expectation of $250 million. They had huge money in the beginning of the year 2000, but were soon going to be broke before the end of that year. The major lesson BS learnt was if you keep spending during the good times, you may be heading for big trouble during bad times. It dawned on him that money is more important than everything else. He claims that if either he or his team were well trained or knowledgeable on the financial front, they could have been more prudent in building a better business much earlier.

The investor then brought in their team to clean up the financial mess Cricinfo was in. It was only after this rough patch that Cricinfo starting making revenue and gradually turned breakeven. They had borrowed loans from their investor for their working capital requirement. There were tough decisions taken to let go some staff, closed offices and cost controls to be effected. They moved to the Indian market due to lesser costs, better market penetration and enabled better technology development.

They still had another battle to fight, as their investor wanted to exit. Luckily, in 2003, they had one cricket company which wanted to buy out 100 per cent. Left with no choice, BS and team yielded to the new buyer's request of wanting only the assets of Cricinfo for GBP 5 million, thus leaving liabilities of more than GBP 4 million for BS and team. With the money obtained, the loans were paid off, and a meagre sum was left for BS and team. Cricinfo merged with the new, bigger company and grew, and BS was an employee of Cricinfo till 2005, after which he started his second venture in publishing.

By 2006, BS has severed all formal ties with Cricinfo. This time around, Cricinfo had new owners yet again. It was sold at a good deal but BS was not a part of it. Although Cricinfo was a brainchild of BS and team, in the end, they did not gain as much.

Opportunity Loss

He summarises what he missed from his entire Cricinfo journey:

- Apart from having product sense, it is extremely essential to have a good financial sense to make different deals.
- A fickle investment model has no inherent worth and, hence, the worth of the company should be built.
- When money is offered, take it and keep part of it for yourself to make more interesting investments.
- Do not assume that more and more money will be obtained.
- Keep costs at a minimum, build a viable product, create sufficient moat and be financially prudent.

- The ability to raise money for themselves as well as for the company and hiring top-class talent is a must.

Recommendations

His suggestion to newbie entrepreneurs:

- Build 2 to 3 different revenue streams.
- Monitor the performance and profitability of each division.
- Capitalise on the successful revenue stream as your primary business.
- Accuracy of the financial data.
- Scrutinise the important data points of your business.
- Raw data is essential to build your accurate business model—hence, store all your data digitally from day one.
- Recalibrate the data points each year.
- Track your costs sensibly.
- Appoint external agencies to survey your industry, competitors and gauge your performance against them on crucial info like their profitability, kind of talent they hire, salary costs, customers' base and so on.

To conclude, BS feels that, in India, there are too many heavy and complex regulations, which are not favourable for an entrepreneur. He further adds that Indian entrepreneurs do not have advantages as compared to the entrepreneurs in the rest of the world due to the stringent regulations to go public or to raise funds and hence essential to have better financial education and learning to deal with venture capitalists.

***

Lifestyle Kingpin Has His Way, Naturally

(C.K. Kumaravel, Co-founder & CEO, Naturals Salon & Spa, Chennai India)

It is seldom that we see someone break off from a family business, turn into an entrepreneur in pursuit of creating their own identity, face failures, re-bounce with grit and become a successful entrepreneur. That is what makes this particular financial journey even more inspiring. Here is the brief roller coaster financial ride of C.K. Kumaravel (CKK), Co-founder & CEO of Naturals Salon & Spa.

His Take on Money

Hailing from the small city of Cuddalore in Tamil Nadu, and having been educated in the Tamil medium, young Kumaravel was taught that being rich and aspiring for financial surplus was not the right mindset. Further, discussion on money matters was taboo within his family. However, over the years, this outlook changed as he realised the importance and need to have money and to utilise it in the right manner.

He sums up his financial ambition beautifully: *"Money is like fuel for your car. It is neither the journey nor the destination. It is just a means of transportation."* According to CKK, even if one wheel of the car has a flat tyre, moving ahead becomes a challenge. He equates the car with entrepreneurship, where he says each division (like finance, marketing, or products) play an important role towards business growth.

Financial Mishaps

During his initial days, CKK assisted his elder brother and claims he did not know the value of money in lakhs, as he would deal only in crores. It was with this attitude that he ventured into his first business venture, which was the herbal hair powder 'Raaga'. Seeking capital was not an issue at that point in time. Being the brother of C.K. Ranganathan of Cavinkare, people believed in him. They had confidence in his entrepreneurial skills, relied on his goodwill and extended credit facility. Banks extended him loans based on his inherited family property.

Soon, his business headed for doom. In hindsight, he realises some of the financial failures that were committed during this period. Here is a summary:

- Wrong belief that more money solves the problem.
- Real operational problems not being addressed.
- Revenue not as per anticipation.

- Costs soared more than expected.
- Not seeking objective and logical solutions.
- Expecting overnight success without providing sufficient time.
- Diversifying too quickly without focussing on the growth of the existing product.
- Lack of connect with the creditors.
- Succumbing to competition.

He regrets that he did not step back to think, identify real operational issues and learn how to resolve them. He also repents that he did not read enough/attend seminars/speak to his network/learn from experts on finance matters.

Moving from Failure to Success

After the failure of the Raaga business, CKK decided to venture into the lifestyle industry and started a beauty parlour in the name of 'Naturals'. Unlike the previous time, getting capital for this venture was not easy. Even to obtain an amount of few thousand rupees was not easy for him at this time, thus making him understand the importance of money. Some people had even blocked him from their contact list.

The initial journey, even after commencing Naturals was not easy. The costs incurred were higher than the revenue earned. Cash flow was a disaster. The outstanding bills were mounting. Society started looking down upon him as a failure. It was at this point that CKK started psyching himself into the fact that it was his business that was a failure and not him. Listening to self-help audiotapes repeatedly helped him tremendously in achieving this state of mind.

Realising that the entire ecosystem is trapped due to corruption, he wanted to overcome it with a scalable business model. That was when he decided to proceed with the franchising model. The second time around, he was very clear with the strategy that each of his business units was to be a separate profit centre, as that would eventually make his venture profitable. He further earned enormous goodwill when he bought over the investment of the eighth Naturals salon franchisee, which was incurring a loss. Thereafter, getting more franchisees was never an issue, as they knew

CKK was reliable and could be banked on. He had a clear policy that the risk was on him but the rewards were meant to be shared with his franchisees.

Thus, business started growing. One of the keys to his success, he feels, is the fact the he knows a little about each business function—operations, finance, marketing and so on—and not vice versa. The top line is now touching Rs. 500 crores and profits are growing.

Financial Growth

His success mantras for this phenomenal growth, especially in financial terms:

- Having self-learnt about finance in a costly manner, he now ensures he has a good financial overview of the entire business.
- He periodically reviews his finance dashboard, prepared by his CFO month on month, with the key areas of focus being revenue, profits, cash flow and the number of salons.
- He also reasons out the variance with his budgets and ensures that budget correction happens periodically.
- The excess cash is invested into new avenues or reserved for a rainy day (like demonetisation and other issues beyond his control).
- If a particular expense is not yielding revenue within 6 months, he ensures the expense is no longer incurred.
- He believes in the BOT (Build-Operate-Transfer) model. Depending on when the new unit becomes profitable, he transfers it.

Here is his advice for new-age entrepreneurs:

- Making money is a right attribute. So inculcate this mindset.
- Keep a constant tab on the financial progress of your business.
- Adequate systems and processes need to be identified and put in place.
- All the stakeholders need to be profitable and your business model should be scalable.
- Small dream is a crime. Dream BIG.

Future Goals

Surprisingly, he does not have a specific revenue target or a profit target. Instead, he wants to focus on:

- The number of new Naturals salons to be opened.
- The number of new jobs he is going to create.
- The number of new women entrepreneurs he is creating in the process.

His short-term goals:

- Creating a thousand successful women entrepreneurs.
- 3,000 salons pan-India.
- Generating 50,000 jobs.
- Manufacturing Naturals products.

Long-term goals:

- Naturals to be the number one salon chain in the world.
- At least 10,000 salons globally.

According to him, by achieving these, incidentally, he will also earn money, which he intends to give back to society. Here is one determined entrepreneur who is living his words and truly dreaming big.

***

If Fresh, It Has To Work

(Girish Mathrubootham, Founder & CEO, Freshworks Inc., California, USA)

His humble beginnings seem to have taught him the art of financial management that seems to be deep-rooted. No wonder he has replicated his learning into his business as well. This hard-core techie even dabbled in the stock market during the early days of his career. Crediting his financial success to the power of saving is the founder of Freshworks (formerly Freshdesk), Girish Mathrubootham (GM).

Learning the Art of Finance

Although his basic financial principles since his younger days emanated from saving, as he grew, he realised he did not want to curb his spending either. Being a good learner, he drew inspiration from his junior colleague. He mastered the art of striking the right balance between saving and spending. GM succeeded in obtaining this balance by opting to invest in Systematic Investment Plans (SIP), which enabled him to spend as well as be secure through his savings in SIPs.

A strong believer in the potential of saving, he credits most of his financial learning to the book *Rich Dad Poor Dad* by Robert Kiyosaki. Going by the principles in this book, he preferred appreciating assets (like land, mutual funds and stocks) to depreciating assets (like vehicles). He would utilise the interest earned from his investments for his expenses and leave the capital portion untouched. These principles helped him to manage his individual wealth.

Art of Investment

During his one-and-half years in the United States, he decided against leading a lavish life style, which enabled him to save well. He wanted to invest his savings. Going by a well-wisher's advice, GM chose to invest in mutual funds as against buying his second apartment. Looking at the real estate boom, he originally thought that he probably had made a wrong choice. However, on hindsight, he feels he did the right thing as his investment in mutual funds grew rapidly and this liquidity helped provide part of the capital for Freshdesk in 2010.

Even when he had just started Freshdesk, he was a cautious player. He set aside a specific amount as a reserve for his family, should the venture fail.

Art of Starting Up

With the thought that his initial capital and meagre revenue from the early years would keep the business going, he was in for a pleasant surprise. Freshdesk received funding for a million dollars within 10 months of operations and, thus, he never felt the pinch of any financial constraint, even in the beginning. Probably that is the reason, he claims, he does not action any specific cost-control measures. His focus is on generating revenue and delivering excellence.

In the formative years, his organisation formulated the pricing strategy based on competitors. They also explored ways to keep the customers happy by pricing low initially as they were yet to create a brand for themselves. They ensured they delivered good quality and kept prices affordable. Once they knew their products were adding substantial value to the customers, they increased the price.

Art of Financial Management

Since he is strong in the principles of financial management, he claims there have been no major financial blunders. As an organisation, he ensures they follow good unit economics and have ensured sustainable growth. He has teams that collate and compute the cost of acquisition of customer, churn ratio, calculating the ratio of marketing costs to cost of acquisition, measuring lifetime value of customer and so on a regular basis, thus extrapolating not only the expected value but also safeguarding scalability.

Going with his saving principle, as an organisation, they invest in safe liquid instruments. They believe in low risk and low return. To mitigate financial risks, GM relies on insurance. In addition, the regular disaster recovery plan (DRP) and business continuity plan (BCP) are in place. GM has ensured that the organisation is financially sound. Should Freshworks be affected by a business cycle downturn, they are all geared up, up to a turnaround time of 5 years.

Success does not seem to have blurred his vision for striving for improvement. When asked about what he would have done differently in the past, he claims he might have employed strategic leadership in finance especially for governing financial processes when the organisation was probably 2 or 3 years old.

Art of Being Focussed

Based on his experience, he would like to recommend that newbie entrepreneurs focus equally on other processes such as finance, HR, legal and so on. He feels that as a newbie CEO/Founder, developing the product (or service) may seem exciting, but the functional aspects of business are equally important as they form critical components to a successful business. While the product (or service) is the core, the other processes are vital too, he emphasises. Once the core is intact, then the functions need to be in place, claims this visionary.

As for his future plans for the organisation, he wants Freshworks to be a billion-dollar revenue company from India in the product start-up space. He further dreams that Freshworks will be one of the few Indian product start-ups to be in NASDAQ. With no specific timeframe in mind for his dream to come true, he says he prefers to go with the flow.

***

The Games People Play

(Harish Suri, Founder Arknemesis Gaming & Nemesis Bistro, Chennai, India)

Setting foot into an untested arena in the Indian subcontinent and being able to offer a unique customer experience was a big challenge that he had to overcome. Yet another hurdle was being able to seek investors who could understand the intricacies of the gaming industry. However, he managed to get by, despite being bootstrapped and also succeeded in being ably supported by his chartered accountant parents in his maiden entrepreneurial venture. Daring to think differently and willing to take the risk is Harish Suri (HS), founder of the state-of-the-art gaming lounge called Arknemesis, and the café Nemesis Bistro.

Revenue Model

When he was just getting started with Arknemesis, HS was initially ridiculed by his well-wishers on the pricing, choice of the city, business model sustainability and the kind of experience he would be able to offer to his customers. Many were sceptical if he could manage to attract customers as they felt the pricing was much higher compared to the smaller gaming joints.

Yet, HS was clear with his vision and business model. He wanted to have multiple sources of revenue, which was a key to the success of the business, as he realised that gaming by itself was not likely to be sustainable in the long run. He knew the business model must ensure a steady source of revenue. Thus, he ensured that the place should to cater to people with different interests. So, he came up with these revenue strategies:

- He capitalised on the fact that a gamer would always have a secondary interest like sports, TV shows and so on. Hence Arknemesis came to be known as the number one screening joint in the city, attracting potential customers.
- He introduced the rule that they would not serve alcohol, and banned smoking in the premises, thus making it kid-friendly and safe and secure for women and families.
- Another revenue stream was hiring their premises for events such as birthday parties, performing artists and so on, which acted as free marketing tool and eventually translated to customers.
- Arknemesis offered voucher sponsorship for schools and colleges for their cultural events, which resulted in a 20 per cent conversion rate.
- HS pitched Arknemesis to corporates as an activity zone, for team-building activities, which ensured that the revenue was ticking.
- Conducting community events where people with different gaming interests got together resulted in conversion.
- The in-house café generated a substantial portion of revenue from both gamers as well as non-gamers.

He realised that, apart from the unique customer experience that he could offer to his customers, the key ingredient was excellent service (both in terms of the equipment and the staff) to ensure a high retention rate. The staff was specifically trained to be patient and teach new gamers and walk-ins, thus growing the gaming culture.

Marketing Spend

Being in the brick-and-mortar business, HS is cautious about digital marketing spend. He limits going overboard on marketing as he feels they rely more on walk-ins and word of mouth. Having tried various marketing experiments, HS is quick to learn from his marketing mistakes. HS is now picky about marketing events, unless they are specific on gaming or reach his target audience.

Break-even

Considering the high investment, HS expects that it would take around 3 to 5 years to pay back from the brick-and-mortar part of the business. He excludes revenue from the event management and gaming consulting to calculate the payback. Although he has had umpteen requests for franchising, he is sceptical about it at this point in time as it is sensitive and he is particular about maintaining the brand reputation. The staff play a key role in the success, even more than the ambience or the gaming system, he asserts. HS substantiates his views by adding that the staff not only need to know the nuances of gaming but also be patient and connect with the customers to build a community of regular customers. Due to this concern of getting the right staff, HS is willing to wait longer to breakeven rather than affect the brand image. Due to the amount of investment into the infrastructure, HS is cognisant of the fact that it would take time to break-even.

Pricing Strategy

After playing it safe initially, HS took a bold decision with the pricing strategy. Being well aware that Arknemesis was priced about three to four times higher than his competitors, HS knew that he had to offer in turn to his customers exceptional service, well trained staff, good gaming systems, and a clean and friendly environment. He also focuses on maintaining the premises well, particularly the toilets. A tip HS provides on his gamble of arriving at the pricing is to talk to the customers, sense their pulse on the offering and seek customer feedback, which seemed to have worked in his favour. HS further offered slab-range pricing from low to high as well as happy hours on the low gaming systems. He also intends to offer coins/vouchers to his regular customers, which they can exchange for a free meal or extra gaming hours.

He regrets having started late in enabling customers to buy the gift vouchers, which also generates more customers in turn. On hindsight, he feels he could have planned the café better by roping in the food and beverage consultants earlier.

His short-term vision for Arknemesis is to get into sport event management and e-sports. Looking ahead, HS intends to move in the direction of event management, take e-sports into the next level and target the international gaming community for gamers.

***

Mask It

(Rajesh K Parthasarathy, Founder, President & CEO, Mentis Software, New York, USA)

It is not common for a chartered accountant to venture in the space of data security and data masking. Yet, Rajesh K. Parthasarathy (KP) dared to explore this terrain way back in the year 2004. Since then, there has been no looking back as Mentis Software, after taking baby steps initially, is now taking giant leaps and is eager to grow further. KP shares his funding journey.

Bootstrapped Start

Having cashed in on his investments and raising further funds from family and friends, KP took the plunge as he had his first customer ready and they had signed up Mentis for a term of 3 years. A few other customers trickled in and, hence, KP let the revenues dictate his investments and shied away from seeking external investors. Apart from the fact that he did not require funding at that point in time, a major reason that drove him towards this decision was the fact that he was quick to realise that the target market for Mentis was not yet ready. Unlike his existing customers, many in the industry were not as forward thinking and had not yet adapted themselves from the compliance perspective, thus not providing much scope for growth.

On hindsight, KP felt it was wise that he did not raise further capital, as he would have been under undue pressure to perform in a place where the market was not ready to receive, and thereby the investors' expectations would not have been met. Further, not many understand about this business and he had limited insight at that point in time as to how the market would pan out. Luckily for him, the market started picking up in the year 2008. However, some of the big names became his competitors. Yet, he managed to beat the biggies as they were relatively new in the space.

Minimal Funding

The growth journey of Mentis has been in phases of 4 years each. During the first 4 years, they had to be bootstrapped while waiting for customers to develop; the second set of 4 years was challenging as the prospective customers wanted to develop their in-house solutions and Mentis had to tread waters carefully. The third set of 4 years was when competition grew, and so Mentis had to manage to sustain itself. However, the last few years have been a game changer for Mentis, as the market is realising the complexity of the issue and companies have started to approach Mentis for their solutions, as they are now recognised as pioneers in this space.

It is due to this growth that KP decided that it was the right time to seek venture capital. While part of it was funded by some angels, he didn't have to go looking for more as Mentis bagged a huge contract from a leading bank in Switzerland despite facing huge competition. This served as huge validation.

Earlier, when KP had approached venture capitalists, he realised that, since they were not fully abreast in the domain of data masking, it seemed challenging for VCs to understand and they found it confusing, especially as Mentis was catering to the B2B segment. Now, with revenue growing, KP has taken a conscious decision to keep funding at a minimum.

Challenges of Funding

One of the challenges KP had to face was the lack of availability of funding in the early days of starting. Further, he wanted the growth and vision of Mentis to be driving the financial engineering and not to be driven by investors. However, he feels it would be good if start-ups could manage to get funded during the initial few months of operations (if they were keen on getting funded) as it helps to scale up faster. He also warned that, sometimes, single big deals keeps one away from raising capital; when the funds are exhausted, the founder is yet again seeking funds or looking for newer deals. It is important to get investors who believe in your venture. In an ideal case scenario, the investors have to be lead generators for the business, claims KP.

Being a chartered accountant, KP resorts to the conservative approach when it comes to financial projections and valuations. He advises newbies to:

- Plan cash flows ahead, have a solid business plan and raise capital in order to overcome cash flow hassles.
- Have investors who also act as mentors from whom you can seek guidance.
- Build network in a sane manner and engage with them.
- Shape a great team to support your growth.
- Inbound lead is more valuable than outbound marketing.
- Not to invest beyond your affordability and to make sure investments are not wasted.
- Work towards earning your salary every day. This needs to be the mindset of the entrepreneur and the early employees.
- Ensure that every dollar spent translates to revenue.

He forewarns that, while raising funds (especially from friends and family), to be selective about choosing the right people.

Prudent Decisions

During the initial days of starting the business, one has to make the right financial decisions like choosing a marketing spend over fancy office furniture, as the marketing spend will give better returns in the form of revenue growth, brand building and so on. Similarly, investing in a good human resource is better than buying a shiny car for the founder. So spending money where it will directly translate towards revenue growth is good. Once the business is established and there exists ample cash flow, better lifestyle choices can follow. Along with the business expansion, the revenues should not only cater to the present but also for a year ahead.

Looking forward, as a first milestone, KP wants Mentis to be valued at 100 million dollars in valuation and thereafter to reach revenues of 100 million dollars in the next 3 years.

***

No Alliance Sought For This Matrimony

(Murugavel Janakiraman, Founder & CEO, Matrimony.com, Chennai, India)

His initial aversion for handling matters of finance underwent a sea change when his board mandated him to cut expenses substantially in order to break-even. It seemed like an impossible task. Yet, the board did not budge. Left with no choice, the matchmaker had to take the plunge into the world of finance. Realising that, if the costs were not controlled, the business would shut down, as a first step, Murugavel Janakiraman (MJ) started to scrutinise each item of cost of Matrimony.com. Within 6 months, he ensured he met the financial target set by his board with regard to the expenses. Since then, he has good control of finances in his organisation.

When it dawned on MJ that the CEO is responsible for all aspects of the business as well as the P&L, he underwent the metamorphosis of a caterpillar to a butterfly. He left no stone unturned when it came to controlling costs, including shutting down of a few verticals that did not fetch sufficient margins. He induced financial discipline within the organisation. He also learnt to read numbers, identify gaps, recognise opportunities and gained insights, which lead to goal setting and detailed financial planning.

Funding for His Venture

Being one of the early start-up ventures, MJ could raise funding without much difficulty, as he was able to demonstrate his passion, his business idea, his leadership team and so on. Moreover, the fact that there was less competition and scope to grow further helped him with raising the funds. MJ also emphasises the fact that hiring persons with good financial knowledge right from the beginning can be a great asset for an entrepreneur.

Ironically, on hindsight, MJ feels that he could have built the business without raising funds, thereby not diluting his share in the business. The reason behind this being the fact that out of the funds raised, almost 90 per cent of the funds were utilised in the non-matrimony verticals such as job portals, automobile portals and property portals, which did not create any value. However, he is quick to add that the dilution enabled him to learn a lot and gain good experience, which he considers valuable, as it has helped him to scale his business.

Steps for Increasing Efficiencies

In order to increase internal financial efficiencies, he introduced the following within his organisation:

- Zero Based Budgeting.
- Periodic review of expenses.
- Financial discipline of paying vendors on time.
- Computing ROI of marketing costs.
- Skilful negotiation with vendors.
- Evaluating alternatives for expenses.
- Controlling people cost.
- Discarding automatic approval processes on recruitment.
- Benchmarking salary costs with industry standards.
- Optimising infrastructure efficiency without compromising user experience.
- Monitoring of segmental P&L.

Pricing

As he was one of the initial players in his domain of matchmaking, he did have challenges when arriving at the pricing. Although there was no specific logic involved, he gradually increased his prices in the beginning. Thereafter, he reduced the frequency of price increase and focussed on increasing the number of customers to grow his turnover.

Cash Management

One of the main reasons many businesses fail is due to lack of cash flow management—hence, a conscious decision he took was to take money upfront from his customers. Therefore, he did not have receivable issues, thus ensuring a positive cash flow. As the business grew, collecting money upfront ensured the business lived within its financial means of the amounts collected. Although there have been instances when he lost business opportunities for seeking the entire amount upfront, he was firm about his decision of receiving monies due right at the start of all transactions, for all verticals.

Views on Diversification

From his experience, MJ feels diversification in early stages of business is not required due to lack of financial capability, lack of leadership team, low market share and so on. Instead, he advises focusing on capturing the market share, improving profitability and developing a core domain—thereafter, diversification is a good idea he feels. He further adds that there is great scope for growth within the existing business for any entrepreneur, and an entrepreneur does not have to go "outside the box" to seek new ideas. The fields adjacent to your business also provide scope for forward integration he claims. He believes in leveraging on the core strength and building other verticals around it.

Brand Building

It is important to build your brand, advises MJ, especially to attract the best talent in the industry. He built his brand by spending heavily on marketing. He ventured into online marketing as well as TV advertisements. As an entrepreneur, one needs to keep learning perpetually, be passionate about the offering and experiment on the various models, to exploit and expand further.

He dreams of making Matrimony.com a long lasting, multi-billion-dollar enterprise that makes a positive difference in millions of people's lives. He also wants to be a financially and socially responsible entrepreneur.

***

Flop, Flip, Focus

(M.V. Subramanian, Co-Founder & Managing Director, Future Focus Infotech Pvt. Ltd.; Director, Native Angel Network; Regional Council Member, Indian Angel Network, Chennai, India)

This is the journey of an entrepreneur who flopped in his initial business ventures. He then flipped over to success by learning from his mistakes, and co-founded Future Focus Infotech Private Limited. He is also an angel investor.

When M.V. Subramanian (MVS) set out as a newbie entrepreneur in 1994, his pockets were full, not with capital but with many ideas to action in the services industry. Despite not having the investment to start his ventures, he became an entrepreneur. Probably that is what has prompted him to become an angel investor now.

I have categorised his views into 4 phases.

Phase One—Seeking Capital

From his umpteen years of experience, he vouches that, in order to obtain capital for any services related business, you have to ask yourself the following:

- Have you identified the problem area that you are going to cater to?
- What is your understanding of the depth of the problem?
- Do you have an appropriate business model to solve the problem?

Once you have convincing answers to the above and, depending on how well you can present your business model to your prospective investors, you are bound to be successful in obtaining the capital, claims this angel investor.

According to MVS, apart from angel investors, there are many individual investors as well as traditional investors, who have the bandwidth to invest in upcoming successful ventures in return for a stake in the business or share of profits. These investors are sometimes the people who usually exist within your own network, and they are even ready to collaborate with you as a partner, he claims. All you need to do is to speak with conviction on how the issue you have identified will be solved by your business model. *Sounds simple, right?*

Phase Two—Pitfalls

When MVS was a new entrepreneur, he had the wisdom to obtain the required capital for all his ventures, yet they failed. What went wrong? The reasons for the failures, each of which led to the other, were:

- Lack of understanding of the business environment.
- Inability to manage the bear and bull phase of business cycle.
- Not having a clue about financial management.
- Inability to manage working capital.
- Cash-negative situation.
- Default in payables.
- Leading to day-to-day operations being affected.
- Resulting in losing the customers, and
- Finally closing the business.

Beware of these potential pitfalls, he warns.

Phase Three—Business Model

Choosing the right business model plays a vital road to success as per MVS. Three simple steps for getting the right business model:

- Does the identified model generate profits?
- Does the model result in a positive cash balance?
- If either of the above conditions is not satisfied, it is probably not the best business model. It may require some financial tweaking to ensure that the first two criteria are met.

Phase Four—Implementation

Once your business model is in place, your success depends on how well you implement and execute the model.

Thereafter, there is no stopping, declares this veteran.

So, how did he manage to become a successful entrepreneur thereafter? Here are his success mantras:

- Educating each department of his organisation on the financial implication of their actions. Making them understand how their role could contribute to the financial growth of the organisation.
- All his major decisions are from the finance perspective.
- No emotional decisions.
- Building leaders from within the organisation.

- Keeping it simple.

Over the years, with experience gained not only in financial management but also in business acumen, if he were to go back in time, he asserts that he would:

- Understand the impact of sharing equity.
- Negotiate better on equity.
- Would have borrowed money instead of raising capital, so that the share of equity is not diluted.

Being a moderate yet aggressive risk taker, his words of wisdom for budding entrepreneurs:

- Follow up on your receivables.
- Have a close watch on your cash flow.
- Do not deviate from compliance matters.
- Remember that collections are not your revenue.
- Have a good understanding of your P&L.
- Know the difference between cash profit and book profit.
- Keep your finances in control right from the start.
- Do not bite more than you can chew—be extra cautious when accepting large orders.

As an angel investor, he defies the thought process of founders. He also enables them to think out of the box by giving them challenging constraints on their business operations.

This adept entrepreneur is also a firm believer of the stock market and likes to think ahead. No wonder he co-founded Future Focus Infotech. His vision is to become a significant digital company in IT staffing space globally.

***

Pressed by A Notion

(Naveen Valsakumar, Founder & CEO, Notion Press Media Pvt. Ltd., Chennai, India)

Identifying a potential gap in the system, a trio started with a capital of about US$50 in 2012. Since then, there has been no looking back. Developing their idea further, they grew gradually. Bootstrapped during their initial phase, all their business decisions were based on the financial potential and, hence, their growth was not aggressive, recalls Naveen Valsakumar (NV), the CEO of Notion Press.

What Not To Do

He reveals some of the bad practices they had resorted to while handling finance during the initial days and warns business not to follow these:

- Eighteen months of cash runway left idle in the bank account instead of deploying it in the business for better returns.
- Despite the business scaling up, the operations team did not follow cash. They failed to understand why they were incurring a loss despite growth. On deeper probing, they discovered that all the profit from book sales was lost due to inventory leakage. Being in the publishing industry, they were printing much more than the requirement, which led to not only poor inventory management but also blocking the working capital and physical space.
- Poor cash collections further aggravated the financial status.
- They lacked financial discipline. The books of accounts prepared only at the year-end, thus not giving them any clue about the financial performance.
- Given the low fiscal discipline, frequent turnaround of financial consultants and overly relying on financial consultants to provide them with insights, they were initially close to being bankrupt. In addition, the icing on the cake was that the founders did not understand finance.

The good thing due to the above fiascos was the fact that it made NV learn the basics of finance, comprehend a balance sheet and present financial numbers to stakeholders. This shift in the financial attitude drove them to a growth of 139 per cent, being cash positive as well as being profitable.

Changes Implemented

Once NV started understanding finance, he started adding some of the good practices to the existing ones as summarised below:

- No cash transactions since the beginning of Notion Press.
- Proper documentation always maintained since inception.
- Re-negotiated the payment terms with suppliers.
- Finance processes put in place (which helped them sail smoothly with the introduction of GST).
- Upon streamlining collections, he ensured that their suppliers got paid ahead of the negotiated period.
- Daily monitoring of cash flow through auto-generated reports.
- Regular tracking of the economic activity within the organisation.
- Business decisions taken after understanding the impact on cash flow. Conscious decision of founders to focus on financial management.
- Monitoring the ageing of receivables and payables and ensuring that the receivables were higher than the payables.
- Building the trust factor with their suppliers by paying them early with cash surplus as well as proactively informing them about potential delays in settling their dues.
- Monthly review of the financial statements along with operational performance reports containing major metrics like top suppliers, top customers, segmental performance and profitability, lead conversion, cost of customer acquisition and so on.
- Delegating and granting independence to division heads to operate up to a certain financial threshold.
- A clear mandate to each division head that they are responsible for the P&L of their division. This was possible by educating the teams on understanding the P&L.
- Inducing each division to achieve excellence thereby increasing productivity and efficiency, which resulted in profitability of the division.
- Generating innovative ideas from teams (such as automation) that help in cost reduction.
- As hiring was initially disproportionate to the growth, all further hiring decisions driven by the P&L as all divisions strived for excellence and wastage reduction.

- Initiating a different strategy by offering customers newer deals and packages.
- Quicker turnaround time without compromising on the quality.

Take on Cash

Apart from the above, NV also emphasises that a start-up does not have to mean burning cash but insists on having a rationale behind each action and learning from past mistakes. Finance is not just the duty of the CFO but more the business owners. Following unit economics rightly helps in growth. As the business scales, he advises to keep track of whether the cash balance or the profitability enhances.

NV claims that the goal of Notion Press is to disrupt the publishing industry and take it away from gatekeepers. Currently, he claims that the industry is disorganised; authors are sometimes not treated well and are not being paid royalty on time, which Notion Press overcomes. NV has two financial goals: One is to reduce the overheads substantially, and the other is to exceed Rs.100 crore in turnover by the financial year 2020.

***

Technology that Fetches

(Prabakaran Murugaiah, Founder & CEO TechFetch.com, Washington DC, United States of America, serial entrepreneur)

The person behind the running of a well-oiled set-up that has been successful for over 12 years is an unassuming man. The set-up is now ready to expand and grow further. With a keen interest to recreate a Silicon Valley, he challenged himself. Thus, in his hometown, Prabakaran Murugaiah (PM), the Founder & CEO of TechFetch.com in USA, started the Tiliconveli Tech Park in Tirunelveli, a small town in the state of Tamil Nadu. Despite umpteen struggles to set this offshore in Tirunelveli, he is keen to prove the success of Tiliconveli in order to inspire other entrepreneurs.

Managing Funding without Investors

Having started techfetch.com in 2006, PM, like most start-ups, was unable to obtain funding. So he took the bold decision of investing his life savings of 9 years into it. He attributes the reason he succeeded, despite not being funded, to planning it well. He anticipated that the venture would not generate revenue for a year, and hence planned his cash flow for 18 months, after which he hoped it would be cash positive. The reality proved to be different. Therefore, he decided that the strength of technology was needed to mitigate the financing risk. Thus, he opted for process automation, focused on a niche market, and attracted the right target audience with minimum staffing. No wonder, over the 12 years of the company growing over 20 times, the staff strength still remains at 30! PM went a step further and decided to develop and build an in-house customised CRM platform in the initial stages itself, as against purchasing it, thereby not only saving cash outflow but also increasing margins over the long run.

Not a Bed of Roses

Techfetch.com did not see much revenue till their eighteenth month of operation. Thereafter, they had almost thousand revenue-generating customers. Till this was achieved, PM did not take home a salary, maintained high financial discipline and lived a frugal lifestyle both personally and professionally, which made him a stronger entrepreneur.

CEO is also The CFO

Like most founders, PM also had his share of financial struggles. Cash is what impacts every decision, as it is the utmost influencer in any business, asserts PM. Cash is what decides the business strategies, hiring team, customer segment, and so on. Therefore, it becomes vital for the CEO to plan the cash flow, deployment and so on, and thereby act like the CFO.

Bold Decisions

PM quotes examples from his past, where he took bold financial decisions and did not shy away from not providing discounts to customers and incorporated a fixed-price model. This even resulted in letting go of certain customers, which PM did not mind, as cash is the key driver of the business.

Another major business decision he took was with regard to the in-house CRM that was built. As it was a good product, he was approached by some to sell it. However, he took a firm decision not to as he was wise to decipher that it was not the core business that he wanted to focus on. While it may seem a tempting proposition to generate extra revenue, PM claims it requires lot of guts to turn it down. Like an eagle, an entrepreneur needs to have a sharp focus to continue the journey.

Win-Win Situation

PM started the tech park in Tirunelveli with the primary objective of incubating companies especially local entrepreneurs, who are helped by providing the facilities, mentorship, technology and seed funding. This tech park also offers to other global organisations to act as a delivery centre, thus creating a win-win situation and creating an ecosystem. PM also acts as a seed investor in companies that are willing to have their delivery centre in the tech park. He participates actively and helps them grow.

While it might seem like a struggle to operate in a tier-2 or tier-3 city, it is more of a mindset in reality, assures PM. Many issues from over a decade have all been resolved now. With an easily trainable workforce, availability of tools, and reduced costs, tier-2 and tier-3 cities are the best for an entrepreneur, according to PM. He also intends to document the dos and don'ts and the challenges and ready to share with other aspirants and showcase Tiliconveli as a pilot example. This further enables job creation, mentoring college students as well as building products around agriculture, mechanisation and so on.

Diversification

According to PM, it is best to diversify at a later stage, once the existing business is well set up and reaches a certain level and fully functional by the next level team. After techfetch.com and Tiliconveli were self-sustained and well managed, he also expanded his entrepreneurial vision into other companies into AI and IOT as a co-founder.

Funding for New Entrepreneurs

Whenever PM is asked about funding of new ventures, he wears his mentor hat and the first thing he asks is, "Why do you need the money?"

He further asks, "What will you do if you do not have the money?" He then encourages the new entrepreneurs to create two business plans—one if they were funded, and one if they were not funded, and asks them to identify the delta, which is the difference that the money is bringing in. By getting funding, he warns that there are more pain points involved, as the entrepreneur is answerable to the investors and has to face brutal questions. While being answerable to investors has its advantages, like being more disciplined, he urges the new entrepreneurs to weigh the pros and cons on whether the money is really required or not, unless it makes a real difference.

Creating an Impact

Being passionate about creating rural jobs, PM says, "Give me a hundred entrepreneurs and I shall create 10,000 jobs in Tirunelveli." And, with these 100 entrepreneurs, PM envisions empowering them so that each of them in turn can create more entrepreneurs.

Being a strong advocate of knowledge sharing, PM does not believe in having financial goals but in creating a meaningful impact, and looks at money only as a by-product. The asset he invests in are people, which uplifts him to higher level. His biggest asset base is human capital, he claims. He also shares his success mantra, which is one hour of exercise every day, one hour of learning daily and one hour of contributing for the community every day without expectations.

Entrepreneurship according to PM is in the DNA, not just a financial outcome but beyond. He reminds that an entrepreneur should think long-term and the journey involves sacrifices to be made.

***

Are Adjustments Required to Be Global?

(Ranjini Manian, Founder and Ex-CEO, Global Adjustments Services Pvt. Ltd., Chennai, India)

While many may be sceptical about starting a new venture, here is a lady bold enough to start a totally new industry in the country. With limited investment, an expatriate partner and a great idea, off she set with the intention to make lives easier for the people who relocate across countries, from and to varied cultures. She is none other than Ranjini Manian (RM), the founder of Global Adjustments. From a small beginning to a five-vertical-strong business, the company has grown manifold.

Relying on A Mentor

When RM set off in 1995, she did not dream of making it this big. Global Adjustments being in the service sector, and a new concept, faced initial resistance in terms of acceptance. At the time of starting, both partners did not have much financial knowledge. They were clueless as to how to go about pricing, as there was neither a benchmark nor an industry standard to follow suit. Thankfully, they had a mentor to their rescue, who insisted against their under-pricing of services that they were rendering. He insisted that their services had to be rightly priced for customers to understand the value of their services.

Independent Verticals

During their initial days, a notebook served for the purpose of income and expenses. A business plan did not exist. After a year, her partner left, as she had to go back to her country of origin. As a single-handed leader, RM grew the business and there were two business verticals—one for relocation and the other was for cross-cultural training. Although not so familiar with handling finance, RM was very clear about basic financial sense. She wanted each vertical to pay for itself and she would apply logic in all her business decisions. She wanted organic growth. Thus, the business grew at a fast pace. Along with the business, she became the brand ambassador for Global Adjustments.

Investing in Premises

Looking back, she feels she could have grown faster if she were not risk averse. She also regrets not thinking big due to the fear of not able to meet financial commitments. However, she is glad that she made the wise choice of investing in her own premises in Chennai. The conscious decision that she did not want to compromise on the brand drove her to this decision. Although it cost her a fortune when she bought it, the values have appreciated manifold.

Business Growth

Before she knew it, the business had 5 successful verticals—all complimenting each other, the new additions being Realty, Publishing and Events. She credits the new ideas to these new revenue streams. However, she also says one needs to look beyond the financial benefit that accrues. Often this leads to intangible benefits, she vouches. She urges entrepreneurs to be forward looking, to believe in their business, take calculated risks and raise their own bar.

One of the testing times was when the business was not accepted as a sustainable and scalable model as it revolved on changing people's mindset about this service. She succeeded on this front by making investments into her business. She also increased awareness by advertising and aligning her company goals of promoting Indian culture with bureaucrats, thus gaining visibility of the business.

Learnings

As a business leader, another challenge she faced was with people management. The mistake she says was that she operated more from the heart than the head. However, she claims it should be other way if you want your numbers to soar fast.

She has also learnt to "Think Abundance", and take decisions in line with this principle. If only she could revisit her past, she says she would have started the pan-India operations much earlier and would have ideally liked Global Adjustments to be headquartered in Delhi or Mumbai.

Over the years, she has also learnt that "Money needs to make more money" and, as a result, invests in mutual funds. Time has made her little less averse to risk. She has further learnt to rely and take expert advice from business consultants and professionals who help her to achieve these.

Healthy Practices

From her vast experience, she shares her words of wisdom for the new-generation entrepreneurs. She recommends that the following practices be inculcated right from the beginning of the entrepreneurial journey:

- De-associate yourself as a brand for the business because, over time, people forget you. However, the brand outlives you.
- Set aside separate time for thinking about your business and growth. Plan your vision accordingly. The time you spend on thinking is what will reward you.
- Develop internal leaders who can take right decisions even in your absence.
- Learn to delegate to your subordinates. Do not over load yourself with everything.
- While you can delegate everything pertaining to operations, do not delegate business development. Because you are the best sales person for your business.

Having handed over the reins of the business to her daughter some time ago, she is now busy pursuing her other passion of empowering women. She does it through the charitable arm of Global Adjustments, which is Global Adjustments Foundation.

***

The Shades of Crayon

(Suresh Shankar, Founder & Director, Crayon Data Pte Ltd., Singapore)

He built a start-up in Singapore without raising any funding and ran it successfully for 9 years. IBM acquired this company, which was named Red Pill. The entrepreneur in him could not remain calm and so had to be reborn. Thus was started Crayon Data, which was also incorporated in Singapore. Suresh Shankar (SS) has subsequently opened a Development Centre for Crayon Data in both Singapore and India. SS shares some of his perspectives for successful entrepreneurship.

Give it Time

SS equates a start-up venture with a bamboo tree. Like the bamboo tree, for the initial 1 to 3 years, usually nothing significant happens. The next couple of years too, pass by with the entrepreneur continuing to water and fertilise the soil of the bamboo. Again, nothing major happens. This is when the entrepreneur tends to give up. However, the entrepreneur needs to persevere with his venture and not quit, claims SS. Because, like the bamboo tree, it is after the "fifth year" when the business soars and scales new heights. However, he cautions that, for start-ups, you can never be sure when this 'fifth year' will take place. It could sometimes be earlier or much later, too, he warns. He reminds that no business model can become an overnight success. During the initial few years, even the Zuckerbergs and the Bansals didn't know they would be as successful, he jokes.

Sustainability

Not all businesses have to be a unicorn (a privately held start-up with a valuation of US$1 billion or more). The majority are the smaller businesses, which are also very successful. Irrespective of the size of the business, an entrepreneur needs to give importance to building a sustainable business—achieve break-even sales, make profits, have sufficient cash flows, invest in the business and grow successfully even without venture capital. Continuing the business with the hope of raising round after round of capital is not a healthy practice, and will not be sustainable in the long run. Even if an entrepreneur decides to opt for external capital, SS forewarns that he/she ensures that the terms be favourable to the entrepreneur. The focus of the entrepreneur should be for generating profits, which will ensure sustainability, rather than raising capital.

In the initial phases, for the business to evolve, it implies sacrificing margins for growth, claims SS. The excess margins are to be reinvested back into the business for further growth. The capital should be utilised in the right way, to propel the growth of the organisation.

Funding

While it does make sense for most businesses to raise capital and focus on growth, before raising the extra capital, SS suggests that the entrepreneur needs to ask himself the following:

- How will the extra capital be utilised?
- How will it allow my organisation to grow?
- By raising a round of capital, how much is the equity going to be diluted?
- Is it worthwhile to dilute?
- How much will the revenue grow by raising extra capital?
- How is your personal financial status impacted?
- How can the business survive without raising the extra funding?

According to SS, fundraising should not be undertaken without having a clear goal, without computing the unit economics and not knowing the path to profitability. When under financial pressure, the entrepreneur tends to take bad business decisions. The trick is to be patient and plan the finance requirements for today, for long haul as well as unexpected events.

Financial Planning

SS opines that the financial requirement, especially for the growth period has to be planned properly, in which case the business can fund itself and not be dependent on external funding. He correlates the growth period to that of running a marathon, as you need the physical as well as the financial stability to sustain over the growth period. The entrepreneur needs to strategise the financial ability, capital requirements, revenue growth, investing plan, plotting the path to profitability and so on. That apart, cash flow planning is essential so that the business does not run out fast.

Growth

An entrepreneur should know to strike the right balance between staying too safe and taking risks. Businesses need to be given the time to grow. Or else, the business engine becomes overheated when the growth is too fast and, eventually, the business will burn out and fail. Finding and retaining good talent poses a challenge for entrepreneurship, clubbed with slow revenue cycle, thus impacting the cash flow. The best way to grow is to get more clients and clients' revenue.

Exit Strategy

SS shares his thoughts from experience on exit strategy. In his perspective, a business should be built to run, sustain and grow. The main motto should be to build a great business and not be exit-dominated. By building a great business, it ensures that there are multiple options to exit, thereby facilitating you to pick the best option. When you have a successful exit, SS claims it is both emotionally and professionally rewarding.

Right now, apart from wanting Crayon to be a significant market player, he dreams of doubling Crayon's business in the next 18 months and tripling it thereafter.

***

When the Flow is Orange

(Suresh Sambandam, Founder of OrangeScape, CEO at KiSSFLOW, Chennai, India)

He claims that this start-up does not have any financial blunders, financial mistakes nor major financial challenges. He attributes this financial success to his commerce background. Of the few minor financial challenges, what Suresh Sambandam (SS) recalls from his initial days at OrangeScape are the delays in obtaining the financial reports from the external consultants and absence of logical thinking among the in-house junior finance staff. Like most new entrepreneurs, he claims that he also was under the mistaken belief that the auditor would take care of all the financial aspects. However, he insists that the onus is on the entrepreneur to handle the finance function.

Monitoring Cash

From inception, SS has been a keen observer of the cash status, even more than the P&L review. The main points of focus on his dashboard, even to date, are his cash flow status, spend on marketing, personnel costs and hosting costs. Mentally, he calculates the gross margin, net margin, the tax and profit, which act as his yardstick in prime decision-making.

Once, during the initial stages of the business, when he did have a cash flow crisis, he sold his car to pay the salaries. The cash crunch arose because of two reasons: They were not collecting from their debtors on time and they were not selling enough. However, as his business evolved with a recurring revenue model, as well as low churn ratio, he claims, he is assured of a certain and quantifiable amount of cash inflow each month. Due to the recurring revenue, the organisation now maintains cash reserves only for a maximum period of 6 months.

Reinvesting Cash

As OrangeScape is offering a good product (KiSSFLOW), his strong ideology is to reinvest the excess cash into his marketing spend, which fetches OrangeScape a growth of over 10 times his spend, thus leading to wealth creation. He boasts of a strong in-house digital marketing team with a successful customer conversion ratio of up to 40 per cent from the qualified prospects. His mantra for success is, "Good product, if not great product, is at the centre of successful company. Marketing drives sales and, as a result, customers come to us constantly—effectively making the flywheel spin continuously."

Marketing Strategy

With any good Business to Business (B2B), Small Medium Business (SMB) or Software as a Service (SaaS) product (or service) in hand, SS asserts that once the product is created, you can market it digitally, thus reaching out to your potential customers, thereby enabling the customers to buy. The key difference he points out is that he is not selling but enabling customers to buy. SS further emphasises that (digital) marketing ought to be a core competency for the entrepreneur, as it drives sales.

Angel Investing

Although not a regular angel investor himself, he values any of the following for his potential investments:

- Good ideas with which he can connect.
- Ideas that resolve issues.
- A familiar/well-known team.
- Relies on his intuition.

He cautions the young generation of entrepreneurs to get the basics of finance right and understand their fiduciary responsibilities. He also reiterates that the responsibility of the business lies on entrepreneur.

For a successful product company, SS claims it is essential to have excellent product management function in place along with competent marketing team who can execute the strategy envisioned by the product management team.

SS foresees a bright future for OrangeScape as they are expanding their market into newer terrains from process flow to Case flow and task flow.

***

Venturing Into A (Uni)que Forte

(Umesh Sachdev, Co-Founder & CEO, Uniphore Software Systems, San Francisco Bay Area, United States of America)

Moving on from the original start-up, backed with good technological skills, entrepreneurial mind-set and a mentor Professor from IIT Madras, the duo took the plunge with their novel concept, their working prototype and a minimum viable product. Their offering, being unique, was welcome and chosen for a government-led seed-funding program through IIT Madras. With this initial capital of $100,000 and within a year of incorporation of Uniphore Software Systems, Umesh Sachdev (US) and his co-founder Ravi Saraogi were ready with their saleable product.

Initial Struggles

During their first board meeting, while the founders were applauded for the technical progress, they were not fully prepared to answer questions on the business model and revenue generation methods. The board further interrogated them on the financial management aspects, to which they did not have readymade answers. It was only then that the fact that revenue is the most crucial factor for the business dawned on the techies. However, they pulled up their socks and worked towards obtaining the revenue by making cold calls, sending emails etc. to prospective customers and thereby seeking sales in the pipeline. With this continued vigour, by the second year of operations, they were able to breakeven.

During the initial phase, while they had an accounting firm capture the transactions into their financial system, finance was largely managed between the two founders. As Uniphore started to grow, US employed a part-time individual to handle the finances of the company as well as prepare the internal processes of payments, collections payroll and so on.

Ready to Fund Investors

Not all start-ups have the privilege of investors evincing interest to fund them. As they were in the exclusive space of speech recognition solutions, Uniphore had angel investors waiting to fund their operations. However, there was a glitch as the investors felt it was not a scalable model. This provoked Uniphore to move into the product space and geographically move beyond India, thus enabling them to obtain funding for a million dollars. This spiked their growth and followed by another round of funding. The new investors had their share of fresh thought processes for Uniphore.

Cash Flow Turbulence

With the changed business model focusing on subscriptions and SaaS, they had not foreseen the negative impact on their cash flow. This led them through a turbulent phase causing delay in effecting payroll and other payments. They also learnt to scrutinise each payment invoice, negotiate and induce cost controls. Eventually they succeeded with moral support from the investors as well as by re-wiring the financial processes.

Having raised four rounds of funding, US looks at finance as a means to make smart decisions and invest in areas of growth. He now focuses substantial time looking for avenues to invest and grow as well as spending little time in controlling costs.

When to Seek Funding

Despite having 100 per cent growth in the past 3 years, as an organisation, Uniphore is conscious about planned and unplanned expenditure. Having witnessed the crests and troughs of the investment cycle, US is of the opinion that funding during the early stage of incorporation might not be the best. He substantiates his viewpoint as, usually at this stage, start-ups lack financial maturity to handle the huge sum of investment received. He also feels that the founders find it difficult to handle the cash flow at this stage of operation. However, he adds that this can be negated if the board members are financially savvy and can guide through the initial phase on the management of funds. He is thankful for having pragmatic and pushy members on his board, who have helped him accelerate the growth of Uniphore.

Investor Management

Dealing with over 80 investors of Uniphore is no mean task. US tries his best to meet the expectations of his shareholders and keep them appraised of the internal developments. With the bigger investors, he is constantly in touch with them and seeking their valuable inputs. He updates the investors of the bad news (if any) almost immediately so that it is not a rude shock later on. He invests about one-fifth of his time engaging with his shareholders and investors as he feels that trust is an important ingredient in building relationships.

Risk Assessment

When faced with any business challenge, before approaching his investors, he ensures he has a plan up his sleeve to tackle the challenge. As he thinks ahead, it helps him to anticipate any unknown risks. He specifically evaluates:

- Market-related risks—by assessing market transitions, technology curve and business disruptions.
- Execution risks—by gauging the key personnel, ensuring there is an alternate plan in place, milestones achievement.
- Financial risks—by protecting the returns, not taking blindfolded decisions and better financial planning.

He further categorises the above risks into short-term, medium-term and long-term, where he analyses the risks in detail, thus trying to mitigate them.

Secrets of Getting Funded

From his perspective, he attributes his successful funding from the angel investors and venture capitalists on the following factors:

- Investors invest in reliable people who are capable of leading the organisation. Having a good attitude, ability and experience helps.
- A well thought out and scalable business model with good leadership in place is essential
- Having the right pitch of selling the company's values to the investors.
- Establishing values to fit investors' thesis.
- Clarity of vision over the long term.

Given a chance, he wishes Uniphore could have penetrated the global markets much earlier, rather than focusing only in the Indian market. Now that they have gone global, US is busy embracing new cultures and trying to establish their brand in other geographies. As founders, they believe in leading the way.

According to US, upcoming entrepreneurs should innovate in areas that will have a massive impact, given that the start-up success ratio is minimal. Also venturing into impactful business becomes easier to seek funding. He is a big advocate of 'Do it yourself before delegating'. Financially, he asserts that, there needs to be right focus on cost control.

Looking forward, he hopes that Uniphore will have a valuation of over a billion dollars and revenues exceeding hundred million dollars.

***

Angels Speak

Here are few thoughts collated from some angel investors on what they look for, the basis of their decision-making, their expectations and so on, regarding a potential investment opportunity.

What the Finance

Rajan Anandan (RA), Managing Director, Google India

Apart from being the Managing Director at Google India, RA is also an active angel investor. The following are some of the items that help the RA decide for or against an entrepreneurial pitch seeking investment:

- An area that RA understands and is familiar with (like technology, software or Internet) is where he will invest.
- A team of 2 or 3 founders (not a single founder) who have the ability, willingness and drive to continue for a long-term through the ups and downs of the company.
- Founders who have been together for a while, with skills complimenting each other (and preferably having at least one tech founder).
- A team that is ready with their prototype or product during the pitch.
- Learning from their previous failures.
- He does not encourage founders hedging their risk through the investors but considers founders who have started off with minimum capital of their own.
- Start-ups, which solve real problems, as opposed to a franchising model.
- The level of market validation, consumer preference and user traction of the start-up aids his decision-making.
- He prefers a minimum 6-month-old bootstrapped start-up before seeking angel investment.

As an investor, he expects that each founding team should build a great company, yet RA is well aware that the odds of success are low and the rate of failure in start-ups is very high. Hence, he does not look for high returns from all of them. However, he adds that there are some of the investments, which give a return of over a hundred times the initial investment. He feels although many start-ups fail, the ones that manage to break out, perform exceedingly well. He prefers to invest in start-ups where he believes in the founders, having great ideas.

As he is pressed for time, he prefers that the founders handle the business operations but is always available when they need help. He occasionally follows up on any ideas for them and wishes to be updated with their periodic performance reports. He also wants to be informed upfront on the bad news.

If the founders feel they have tried, tested and yet failed, he understands, tries to counsel them if required, if not help them shut door and move on. He does not lose sleep over such issues.

RA does not have a particular exit strategy in mind but if an awesome company has been built, then the options of exit are many he claims. Rather than focusing on exit, he prefers to focus on great entrepreneurs and be supportive in making them more successful.

***

V. Shankar (VS) – (Executive Committee Member, The Chennai Angels, President of TiE Chennai and Founder of Computer Age Management Services Pvt. Ltd. (CAMS)).

Unlike earlier days, when external sources of funding were a rarity, currently obtaining funding is the least of the worries for an entrepreneur, claims VS. When he started his entrepreneurial journey, he was pragmatic, frugal and bootstrapped, and all profits earned were deployed towards growth.

From his many years of experience, some of the takeaways that VS likes to share with the new generation of entrepreneurs are:

- Not to take external capital in a loose manner unless major growth is foreseen, and to have a good line of sight ahead. He reminds that new investors imply loss of control, space and exit of the promoter eventually. Therefore, organisations should aim at being self-sustaining. Entrepreneurs should not be under the impression that capital is cheap as the excess capital is likely to get eroded with time. An entrepreneur should learn to live within his means and be disciplined from inception. Capital should be utilised into targeted and focussed growth.
- As an angel investor, he looks for:
    - An individual who is committed to the business.
    - His/her knowledge of the business.

- Brings value-add by solving customer issues.
- Integrity of the individual.
- Willingness to learn.
- Ability to be mentored.
- Potential for scalability, potential for raising further capital and potential for exit.

- As an angel investor, he prefers to exit at the series at B-stage
- According to VS, an angel investor invests either for quasi-emotional reasons to support the young entrepreneur in their early stage of business or as an asset allocation strategy seeking reasonable returns. Thus, the exit strategy of each angel investor varies according to their purpose. As an angel investor, VS seeks to raise the level of the start-up by a few notches, exit and thereafter to fund other start-ups, thereby being a catalyst for the growth of many start-ups.
- As start-ups start to scale, entrepreneurs have to make space for other similar calibre professionals as they bring in diverse point of view.
- The aim of the entrepreneur should be to create a successful business. Valuation is the result of successful business, not the target of a business. Thus, the entrepreneur needs to bear in mind that valuation is only the by-product of a successful business and not the objective.
- The business should be what the entrepreneur has invested in conceptually, and not start a business for the sake of starting or replicating a successful business from another geography. The aim should be to create value. With the right background and knowledge, an entrepreneur can create a niche in their area of expertise, thereby creating the recipe for success. Start your venture for the right reasons, cautions VS.
- Delay third-party funding as much as possible, for better valuation reasons.
- It is important to manage cash flow as well as pay the statutory liabilities; not advisable to defer statutory liabilities, as penalties for non-compliances are high.

- VS's horizon as an angel investor is 4 years, within which he feels the start-ups should have made a substantial progress.
- Essential to create a network or be part of a network where ideas can be bounced or exchanged amongst peers.
- If the start-up's ideas have not scaled as envisaged, it is fine to call it a day and either develop another idea or even get back to working for an organisation for a few years before restarting.
- Better to approach angel investors after getting the first round of investment from family and friends.

I trust the above real-life finance stories would have energised you and that you would have learnt more on how to handle your business finance by reading the above inspiring stories. You can learn from their rich expertise and inculcate whatever is applicable to your business. My best wishes for your excellent and maximum financial growth of your business.

The main essence of the book is completed with this. In the next section I have listed some basic finance terms that you need to be aware of as an entrepreneur. It is more like a finance glossary, aimed at providing you a better understanding.

Chapter 10

WHAT YOU NEED TO KNOW

As an entrepreneur, you are expected to know these basic finance terms. If you are familiar with these terms and practices, please feel free to skip this. The terms that are being covered here are:

- Capital
- Assets
- Liabilities
- Equity and Debt
- Financial Statement
- Net worth
- Depreciation
- Net Profit
- Overdraft
- Breakeven
- Unit economics
- Capital expenditure and operating expenditure
- Basic steps for starting
- Chart of accounts

I am presenting these basic finance related terms in a simple manner, as these are essentials a businessperson should know. These are not only required for better financial understanding but also because these are commonly used terms by investors, bankers, board and any other individual or organisation involved with your business.

Capital

"What is required to start your business and keep going."

Capital is the amount invested into the business. It can be in the form of cash (including bank balance), assets and so on. Therefore, it is the owner's investment in the business.

The profit made from the business is known as returns. The returns as a percentage of the capital are known as **Return on Capital employed or ROCE** (also known as ROIC or Return on Invested Capital).

The amount of money that you have borrowed or invested as the capital has a cost attached to it, which is known as the Cost of Capital (COC). This cost is usually the interest cost on the amount that has been invested. The difference between the COC and ROCE is known as spread. When the ROCE is greater than COC, it is said to be positive spread and the vice versa is negative spread.

For example:

If the profits earned are Rs. 10,000, and

the amount of investment is Rs. 100,000 (comprising of Bank balance of Rs. 50,000 for the business operations and computer costing Rs. 50,000),

then, the return on capital employed is 10 per cent, computed as:

$$ROCE = \frac{\text{Profits of Rs.10,000}}{\text{The total investment of Rs.100,000}} * 100 = 10\%$$

Continuing the above example, if the amount of Rs.50,000 is borrowed at an interest of say 8 per cent, the COC is Rs.4,000. Here as the ROCE is greater that COC, it is a positive spread.

Even if you have not borrowed funds from the bank and have invested (maybe) from your savings, you can still compute the notional interest on the amount invested to ensure that the spread is positive, as negative spread does not make financial sense over a period of time.

The capital that a business requires for its day-to-day operations is known as Working Capital. WCR is the abbreviation for Working Capital Requirement. It is the difference between the current assets and current liabilities. Working Capital is a financial metric that denotes liquidity position of the business. Working Capital management is essential to ensure continuous business operations.

Assets

"What adds value to your business."

Assets refer to the economic resources a business owns or controls. Assets are the key drivers used to generate revenue for the organisation. Assets held to generate revenue to the business are commonly known as PPE—property, plant and equipment (also known as Fixed Assets). Assets held for value appreciation as an investment are known as other financial assets, (such as shares or bonds), and property held for revenue generation or capital appreciation is known as Investment Property.

Assets can be tangible assets in the form of computers, vehicles, software, land, buildings, inventory, or bank balance, or intangible assets like goodwill, patents, or copyrights. Assets are reflected in the balance sheet of the entity.

Assets can be classified as non-current assets (for example, property, plant, equipment, investments, which will be used by the entity for more than one year) or current assets (such as cash and bank balance, accounts receivable, inventory, which will be used by the entity within the next 12 months).

Liabilities

"What your business owes. Whatever needs to be repaid."

A liability is a monetary obligation or monies owed arising during the course of business operations. It is a legal responsibility on the organisation, and it is in lieu of the services received or purchased, based on the past transactions or events. It includes debts, bank overdraft, amounts owed to suppliers, provisions, accruals, loans, and so on.

Liabilities can be current liabilities (i.e. immediate debts which need to be settled within the next 12 months) or long-term liabilities (or non-current liabilities).

Retained earnings are the cumulative profits that a company has earned to date, less any dividends or other distributions paid to investors. Retained earnings (also known as accumulated reserves and surplus) are reflected as part of the shareholders equity and are considered as a liability as it is an amount that has to be settled in case of sale.

The difference between assets and liabilities is the owner's equity.

Equity and Debt

"Equity – What is the level of ownership.

Debt – What is the loan repayable by your business."

Both the options refer to a method of funding the operations of the business.

Equity (which is another term for capital) requires raising money by selling the interests in the venture. Equity market refers to the stock market. For example, when you purchase some shares of a company, you hold a part of the stake in the company and thereby a part owner of the company.

The capital requirement of the business is normally funded through any of the following ways:

- When the equity of the business is funded by the entrepreneur's own resources or company's own revenue, the business is said to be bootstrapped.
- When an individual provides a small amount of capital to a start-up in return for a stake in the business, the individual is known as an angel investor. Usually, angel investing precedes a seed round and happens during the infancy stage of the start-up.
- Venture Capital (VC) refers to the amount provided by Venture Capital firms to small, high-risk start-ups, with major growth potential.

Debt on the other hand involves the amount borrowed for the purpose of working capital or capital expenditure that has to be repaid later along with interest. It could be in the form of bonds, bills, notes, loan and so on. Income tax benefit on interest paid on debt is available.

Debt is fundamentally more risker than equity, as sometimes, the business tends to live beyond its means. Hence, extra care, caution and prudence is to be applied while opting for debt as a means of financing.

If the debts taken are more than you can handle, you may be headed for disaster. One of the main reasons why the giant store Toys R Us, the king of toy castle, filed for bankruptcy, as it could not handle its heavy debt.

Financial Statement

"What is your financial position."

Financial statements represent certain statements prepared to reflect the financial performance (income statement), financial position (balance sheet) and summary of cash flow for a defined period of time. Thus, it provides financial insight into the business. It is a summary of the financial activity of the business or entity for a given time period. It comprises of mainly the Income statement, balance sheet and cash flow statement. While the income statement and cash flow are over a period of time (say 6 months or a year), balance sheet reflects the financial position as on a particular date (say as on 31 March of a particular year). Cash flow statement reflects the movement of cash in and cash out for a particular period.

Financial statements are usually prepared as per the Generally Accepted Accounting Principles (GAAP) as suggested by the respective jurisdiction. In India, we need to prepare financial statements in line with Indian Accounting Standards (IAS) and, for some companies, as per International Financial Reporting Standards (IFRS). As per IFRS, income statement is known as Statement of Comprehensive Income and balance sheet is called Statement of Financial position.

Auditors utilise the financial statements for the purpose of conducting an audit, and investors (and prospective investors) utilise financial statements to gauge or measure the financial progress of the entity from the viewpoint of investing or financing a business. Regulators also read the financial statements to regulate based on the statute they are governed by. For example, an income tax officer will use a financial statement to identify the amount of corporate tax the company needs to pay.

Net Worth

"What is the difference between what you own and what you owe."

Net worth is the excess of assets over liabilities. Net worth can be calculated for both a business as well as for an individual. It is the value that is owned by the entity minus the debts owed. It is used as a measure to compute the value of the business.

A high net worth implies a high financial strength and also a good credit rating.

HNI refers to High Net worth Individuals.

Net worth is also known as shareholders equity. The simplest formula to calculate net worth is:

> Total assets − Total liabilities = Net worth

Another way to calculate net worth is the sum of Share Capital and accumulated reserves and surplus.

While seeking funding from the investors (or potential investors), one of the areas of decision-making of the investors could be the net worth of the business.

Depreciation

"What is the decrease in value due to age and use."

Depreciation is the reduction in the value of an asset over time due to its wear and tear. Depreciation is a mandatory charge under the Companies Act. This charge does not involve any cash outflow. It is an allowable expense for Income tax purposes. Through depreciation, the value of the asset is written off over time.

Depreciation can be claimed only as long there is a useful life for the asset. Once the asset is fully depreciated, no more depreciation can be claimed. Depreciation appears as an expense in the P&L account. The net amount after charging the depreciation is known as the Net Book Value (NBV).

For example:

If the cost of a computer is Rs. 60,000 and is depreciated over 4 years, the depreciation charge each year is:

$$\frac{\text{Cost of Asset (Rs.60,000)}}{\text{Expected Life (4 years)}} = \text{Rs.15,000}$$

Therefore, Rs. 15,000 is the depreciation for each year for 4 years. At the end of year one, the value of the asset (which is the NBV), reflected in the Balance Sheet is Rs. 45,000; NBV end of second year at Rs. 30,000; and NBV end of third year at Rs.15,000. From the fourth year onwards, the value of the asset is NIL and the computer is then classified as a fully depreciated asset.

This method of calculating depreciation is known as straight line method, which is used commonly. Another way depreciation can also be calculated is known as the written down value method, where the NBV is depreciated year after year (instead of the cost of the asset).

If, in the above example, the computer is sold at the end of the fifth year for Rs.10,000, this amount of Rs.10,000 is shown as profit on disposal of asset. If the asset is sold for a value lesser than its NBV, it is shown as loss on disposal of asset. Should an asset be lost, damaged or stolen, the entire book value is deemed as loss.

| Sale price of asset – Book value of asset = Profit on disposal of asset. |

Net Profit

"What you sell minus what you spend."

Net profit or net earnings of the entity is commonly known as the bottom line. It is the difference between the total of all the revenues and the total expenditure. The expenses that are to be included while computing the bottom line include the cost of sales, administration expenses, and other charges like interest, depreciation and taxes.

Some of the commonly used abbreviations include:

EBITDA – Earnings before Interest, tax, Depreciation and amortisation

EBIT – Earnings before Interest and Tax (also known as Operating Profit)

EAT – Earnings after tax (also known as PAT—Profit after tax)

NP – Net Profit

PBIT – Profit before interest and tax

Top line indicates the gross sales or the revenue of the business.

All businesses aim at increasing their bottom line. This can be achieved by increasing the top line and/or building efficiencies by reducing the costs.

Overdraft Facility

"What is the amount you can utilise even if you do not have the amount."

Overdraft facility is a facility that can be provided by your bank. It is a facility where your bank will allow you to draw cash over and above your available cash balance from your current account up to the approved overdraft limit. It is a credit facility extended to you by the bank. It is repayable upon demand from the bank.

In return for extending this facility, the bank will seek a security and charge you interest on the amount over drawn. The overdrawn amount is reflected as liabilities in your balance sheet.

The main advantages of opting for the overdraft facility is that it comes in handy at the time of a cash crunch and allows you to maintain a good track record of your payments.

On the flip side, you are charged with high interest costs and this might make you lethargic in following up for payments with your debtors.

If you have decided to opt for the overdraft facility, do remember to shop with a few banks that are willing to extend this facility to you and do negotiate for the best terms and conditions.

Cash credit is a facility of borrowing without having a credit balance and is limited to the extent of borrowing limit fixed by the bank. The difference between cash credit and overdraft is on the security offered and whether the money is lent out of a separate account.

Break-even Point

"What happens when income equals expenses."

This is the point where there is no profit or loss for the business. In other words, the total cost equals the total revenue.

So, how do you compute the break-even point? Let us take this example. Your organisation is a service provider.

- Your monthly fixed costs are Rs. 8,00,000.
- Each of your resource generates revenue of Rs. 100,000 per month and the corresponding variable cost for each is Rs. 60,000.
- To arrive at the contribution:

  > Sale price – Variable cost = Contribution

  Therefore, your contribution is Rs. 40,000.

- In order to compute your break-even point or in other words, the minimum number of resources you need to employ to arrive at a no profit or no loss situation will be:

$$\text{Break-even point} = \frac{\text{Total fixed cost (Rs. 800,000)}}{\text{Contribution (Rs. 40,000)}} = 20$$

By arriving at the break-even point, you will know that you have to employ more than 20 resources to start making profits. To understand it better, let us view from the other side.

Scenario 1: Suppose you have 22 resources working for you, generating revenue of Rs. 100,000 each per month.

Therefore, your total revenue is Rs. 22,00,000.

The total variable cost for the 22 resources amounts to Rs. 13,20,000 (Rs.60,000 * 22 resources).

Contribution = Rs. 22,00,000 − Rs. 13,20,000 = Rs. 880,000.

Profit = Contribution of Rs. 880,000 − fixed costs of Rs. 800,000 = Rs. 80,000.

Scenario 2: Let us say you have only 15 resources.

Revenue − 15 * 100,000 = Rs. 15,00,000

Variable costs − 15 * 60,000 = Rs. 900,000

Contribution = Rs. 600,000

Less : Fixed costs = Rs. 800,000

Net loss − Rs. 200,000

Thus, employing more than 20 resources will lead you towards profitability.

By computing and analysing your break-even point, you can determine the minimum quantity you need to sell to cover all your costs.

> Total profit at break-even point is zero.

Break-even point can be helpful in computing project profitability, determining the selling price, arriving at the minimum level of sales and so on.

Unit Economics

"What is the power of one."

Entrepreneurs need to be wary of this term, as it can make or break your business, especially as it is helpful in analysing the performance of your business and also predicting the future growth potential.

Unit economics denotes business performance. When the direct costs and revenues of a particular business model are expressed in terms of each unit, it is unit economics. When the unit revenue is more than the unit cost, you make a profit. Unit economics is an indicator of whether you are earning profit on each unit that you are selling.

If you are a product company and the cost of each product is Rs. 600 and the sales value of each product is Rs. 1,000, the profit per unit is Rs. 400. This is also referred to as contribution or margin.

However, if you are a service company, unit economics is calculated differently. The cost is computed (or referred) as Cost per Acquisition (CPA, also known as CAC—Customer Acquisition cost), which refers to how much it costs to acquire a customer. This is compared with the Lifetime Value (LTV) of a customer. LTV is the amount of revenue generated by each customer during their entire duration as your customer. LTV is also known as CLV (Customer Lifetime Value).

Few other related terms that you would like to note are:

TAM: Total Available Market (which denotes the total market demand)

SAM: Serviceable Available Market (is a segment of TAM that forms part of your target)

SOM: Serviceable Obtainable Market (which is the portion of SAM that you can capture)

MQL: Marketing Qualified Lead (is a website visitor whose engagement levels indicate when the likely conversion as a customer will happen)

SQL: Sales Qualified Lead (refers to a prospective customer as per the organisations' marketing department and then by the sales team and is deemed ready for sale)

As an entrepreneur, you need to understand the various metrics that impact the unit economics. This is specific to your business.

> The goal should be to minimise the CPA and maximise the LTV for better unit economics.

Depending on the nature of your business, you may also wish to compute average monthly revenue per customer, identify your revenue drivers, customer conversion rate, cost per online visitor and so on, for your unit economic analysis.

By understanding the unit economics of your business, you can take the right business decisions and also tweak your business model as required, to ensure sustainability and generation of profits.

Remember that prospective investors will prefer when the unit economics of your business is positive, as they will regard it as a high potential business to invest in, thus making it a viable investment opportunity.

Some of the other related terms used in this context include:

- MRR—Monthly recurring revenue: This refers to the amount of revenue that is certain and will recur month after month.
- Customer churn rate: This refers to the percentage of customers who are no longer your customer thus denoting the attrition rate. It reflects the rate at which you are losing your customers or the rate at which the customers are no longer subscribing to your services. A churn rate of 25 per cent implies an average customer lifetime of 4 years.

To calculate churn rate, the formula to be applied is:

(Customers at the beginning of the month – Customers at end of the month)/Customers at the beginning of the month.

For your business to grow, the number of new customers must exceed your churn rate.

Unit economics can be useful in financial decision making, calculating the ROI and forecasting the future profitability of the business.

Few other commonly used terms and abbreviations:

- B2B – Business to Business
- B2C – Business to Customer
- BOD – Board of Directors
- OD – Overdraft
- IPO – Initial Public Offer
- NDA – Non-Disclosure Agreement
- POC – Proof of Concept
- MIS – Management Information System
- MSA – Master Service Agreement
- SMB/SME – Small Medium Business/Small Medium Enterprise
- SOW – Statement of Work

- SaaS – Software as a Service
- VC – Venture Capital

Capital Expenditure And Operating Expenditure

"Capital expenditure: What is the asset.
Operational expenditure: What is required to run your business operations."

Expenditure incurred towards purchase of any assets like computers, land, building, software, vehicles, or equipment, are known as capital expenditure or capex. It can also pertain to expenses that are incurred towards the acquisition of assets or investments by the organisation. Capex helps towards increasing the operations of the business.

The capital expenditure is usually written off over a period of time, say 3 to 5 years. This is determined by the internal policy of the organisation, which is usually in line with the useful life of the asset. Therefore, the impact of capital expenditure on the P&L is to the extent of the charge by way of depreciation for each year. Note that the impact of capital expenditure on the cash flow is indeed the full amount.

Capital expenditure is different from operating expenditure. Operating expenditure (opex for short) is incurred for the day-to-day operations and it is also known as revenue expenditure. They are short-term expenses in nature.

The amount of capital expenditure for an organisation requires depends on the organisation's operations and the industry it operates in. When the capital expenditure is high, the organisation is known as capital-intensive organisation.

Basic Steps for Starting a Business

Listed below are some basic steps that are required to be in place for starting of any business in India. This is to give you an idea for the requirements.

Please note that this is only an indicative list. Please check on the latest rules and regulations when you are starting up.

- Obtain PAN (Permanent Account Number).
- Open a current account with a bank.

- Obtain TAN (Tax deduction and collection Account Number), GSTIN (GST Identification Number), professional tax registration and so on.
- Register trademark/patent.
- If you are starting a company, obtain a company seal.
- If employing more than 20 persons, register for PF (Provident Fund).
- If employing more than 10 persons, register for ESI (Employee State Insurance).
- Register for GST (Goods and Services Tax).
- Register under respective State's Shops and Establishment Act.
- If foreign capital is involved, get necessary Reserve Bank of India approval.
- If you are having leased office premises, get it registered with the respective sub-registrar
- If it is partnership form of business, execute a partnership deed or register a Limited Liability Partnership (Limited Liability Partnership is a new corporate structure that combines the flexibility of a partnership and the advantages of limited liability of a company at a low compliance cost).
- If starting a private company, acquire DIN (Directors Identification Number) for directors; ensure there are required number of shareholders, share capital and so on.
- Obtain DSC (Digital Signature Certificate) for directors.
- Prepare Memorandum and Articles of Association.
- Apply for name availability of your company.
- Get incorporation documents stamped and filed.
- Register with Registrar of Companies (ROC) to obtain incorporation certificate.
- Register under Micro, Small and Medium enterprises (MSME) Act if it is applicable.

If you are starting outside of India, check on the local requirements of that country.

Chart of Accounts

Irrespective of the industry you are in, here is a sample chart of accounts that you can create from the accounting perspective. You may customise it further to suit your requirements.

For ease of working, the main areas of assets, liabilities, income and expenditure are grouped together under each of these main headings and sub grouped thereafter.

This classification of the chart of accounts will also give you an idea of the different nature of assets, liabilities, income and expenses.

Notice how there is a main account number, which has a sequence of sub accounts for further classification. The sub-account classification is applicable only for those accounts that you want to sub-divide. For example, depreciation is the main account and the depreciation of the various categories of the assets comprise of the sub-accounts.

For better understanding of your costs, if required, you can also include a column for 'Cost Centre' in the chart of accounts. A cost centre is a department within your organisation. The manager and employees are responsible for the cost that it generates costs but and not revenue. It could be a location, person or an item. It can also be a production cost centre or a service cost centre.

The common responsibility centres are cost centre, revenue centre, profit centre and investment centre.

Sl No	Grouping	Sub Grouping	Main Account No	Sub Account No	GL Name
1	Assets	Bank	1009	000	Bank Balances
2	Assets	Bank	1009	001	Bank Account 1
3	Assets	Bank	1009	002	Bank Account 2
4	Assets	Bank	1009	003	Fixed Deposit
5	Assets	Cash	1025	000	Cash Balances
6	Assets	Cash	1025	001	Petty Cash
7	Assets	Cash	1025	002	IOU Account

Sl No	Grouping	Sub Grouping	Main Account No	Sub Account No	GL Name
8	Assets	AR	1032	000	Accounts Receivables—Domestic
9	Assets	AR	1032	001	Customer 1
10	Assets	AR	1032	002	Customer 2
11	Assets	AR	1033	000	Accounts Receivables—Global
12	Assets	AR	1033	001	Customer 1
13	Assets	AR	1033	002	Customer 2
14	Assets	AR	1036	000	Unbilled Receivables
15	Liability	Provisions	1038	000	Provision for Doubtful Debts
16	Assets	Advances	1051	000	Advances
17	Assets	Advances	1051	001	Travel Advances
18	Assets	Advances	1051	002	Other Advances
19	Assets	Advances	1051	003	Advances to Suppliers
20	Assets	Advances	1051	004	Advances to Employees
21	Assets	Accruals	1055	000	Accrued Int. on Demand Deposit
22	Liability	Taxes	1069	000	Output GST
23	Liability	Taxes	1069	001	Output CGST
24	Liability	Taxes	1069	002	Output SGST
25	Liability	Taxes	1069	003	Output IGST
26	Assets	Deposits	1077	000	Deposits
27	Assets	Deposits	1077	001	Rental Deposits
28	Assets	Deposits	1077	002	Other Deposits
29	Assets	Advances	1082	000	Prepaid expenses
30	Assets	Taxes	1093	000	Taxes
31	Assets	Taxes	1093	001	TDS deducted by Customers
32	Assets	Taxes	1093	002	TDS on Interest Income
33	Assets	Taxes	1093	003	Advance Tax
34	Assets	Taxes	1093	004	Deferred Tax Assets

WHAT THE FINANCE

Sl No	Grouping	Sub Grouping	Main Account No	Sub Account No	GL Name
35	Assets	Fixed Assets	1302	000	Fixed Assets
36	Assets	Fixed Assets	1302	001	Office Equipment
37	Assets	Fixed Assets	1302	002	Computers
38	Assets	Fixed Assets	1302	003	Vehicles
39	Liability	Acc. Depreciation	1401	000	Accumulated Depreciation
40	Liability	Acc. Depreciation	1401	001	Accumulated Depreciation—Office Equipment
41	Liability	Acc. Depreciation	1401	002	Accumulated Depreciation—Computers
42	Liability	Acc. Depreciation	1401	003	Accumulated Depreciation—Vehicles
43	Liability	AP	2003	000	Accounts Payables
44	Liability	AP	2003	001	Vendor 1
45	Liability	AP	2003	002	Vendor 2
46	Liability	Taxes	2023	000	Dividend Distribution Tax
47	Liability	Taxes	2024	000	TDS Payables
48	Liability	Taxes	2024	001	TDS on NRI Payments
49	Liability	Taxes	2024	002	TDS on Contractors
50	Liability	Taxes	2024	003	TDS on Professional Fees
51	Liability	Taxes	2024	004	TDS on Rent
52	Liability	Taxes	2024	005	TDS on Salaries
53	Liability	Govt Dues	2031	000	Statutory Dues
54	Liability	Govt Dues	2031	001	PF (Employees') Contribution
55	Liability	Govt Dues	2031	002	PF (Employer's) Contribution
56	Liability	Govt Dues	2031	003	Profession Tax Payable
57	Liability	Govt Dues	2031	004	Employee's Contribution to ESIC

Sl No	Grouping	Sub Grouping	Main Account No	Sub Account No	GL Name
58	Liability	Govt Dues	2031	005	Employer's Contribution to ESIC
59	Assets	Taxes	2042	000	Input GST
60	Assets	Taxes	2042	001	Input CGST
61	Assets	Taxes	2042	002	Input SGST
62	Assets	Taxes	2042	003	Input IGST
63	Liability	Provisions	2066	000	Provisions
64	Liability	Provisions	2066	001	Provision for Tax
65	Liability	Provisions	2066	002	Provision for Audit Fees
66	Liability	Provisions	2066	003	Provision for Professional Fees
67	Liability	Provisions	2066	004	Provision for Performance Incentive
68	Liability	Provisions	2066	005	Provision for Salaries
69	Liability	Provisions	2066	006	Provision for Leave Encashment
70	Liability	Provisions	2066	007	Provision for Gratuity
71	Liability	Provisions	2066	008	Provision for Expenses
72	Liability	Provisions	2066	009	Proposed Dividend
73	Liability	Liability	2203	000	Revenue billed in advance
74	Liability	Loans	2213	000	Other Long-Term Loans
75	Liability	Share Capital	2302	000	Capital & Reserves
76	Liability	Share Capital	2302	001	Share Capital
77	Liability	Share Capital	2302	002	Securities Premium
78	Liability	Share Capital	2302	003	General Reserves
79	Liability	Share Capital	2302	004	Profit & Loss Account
80	Income	Income	3003	000	Revenue
81	Income	Income	3003	001	Revenue—International
82	Income	Income	3003	002	Revenue—Domestic
83	Income	Income	3101	000	Interest on Deposits
84	Income	Income	3104	000	Other Income/(Expenses)
85	Income	Income	3105	000	Exchange Gains/(Losses)

WHAT THE FINANCE

Sl No	Grouping	Sub Grouping	Main Account No	Sub Account No	GL Name
86	Income	Income	3105	001	Realised Gains/(Losses)
87	Income	Income	3105	002	Unrealised Gains/(Losses)
88	Expense	Taxes	3191	000	Income Tax
89	Expense	Taxes	3191	001	Deferred Income Tax
90	Expense	Taxes	3191	002	Current Income Tax
91	Expense	Taxes	3191	003	MAT Credit Entitlement
92	Expense	Expenses	4002	000	Outsourcing Staff fees
93	Expense	Expenses	4005	000	Software Maintenance Expenses
94	Expense	Expenses	4008	000	Postage and Courier
95	Expense	Salary	4103	000	Salary
96	Expense	Salary	4103	001	Bonus
97	Expense	Salary	4103	002	Basic
98	Expense	Salary	4103	003	House Rent Allowance
99	Expense	Salary	4103	004	Special Allowance
100	Expense	Salary	4103	005	Relocation Allowance
101	Expense	Salary	4103	006	Performance Awards
102	Expense	Salary	4103	007	Conveyance Allowance
103	Expense	Salary	4103	008	Leave Travel Allowance
104	Expense	Salary	4103	009	Medical Expenses Reimbursement
105	Expense	Salary	4103	010	Other Allowance
106	Expense	Salary	4103	011	Referral Salaries
107	Expense	Salary	4103	012	Notice Period Pay
108	Expense	Salary	4103	013	Stipend
109	Expense	Salary	4103	014	Employer's Contribution to ESIC
110	Expense	Salary	4103	015	Vehicle Reimbursement
111	Expense	Salary	4103	016	Employer's Contribution to PF
112	Expense	Salary	4103	017	Gratuity Expenses
113	Expense	Salary	4103	018	Leave Encashment

Sl No	Grouping	Sub Grouping	Main Account No	Sub Account No	GL Name
114	Expense	Salary	4103	019	Labour Welfare Fund
115	Expense	Expenses	4203	000	Employee Relocation Expenses
116	Expense	Expenses	4205	000	Recruitment expenses
117	Expense	Expenses	4222	000	Meetings-Food/Beverages
118	Expense	Expenses	4224	000	Canteen Beverages
119	Expense	Insurance	4232	000	Medical Insurance
120	Expense	Expenses	4235	000	Team building expenses
121	Expense	Expenses	4237	000	Other Staff Welfare Expenses
122	Expense	Expenses	4239	000	Food vouchers
123	Expense	Expenses	4304	000	Security Charges
124	Expense	Travel	4334	000	Travel
125	Expense	Travel	4334	001	Auto/Taxi/Bus
126	Expense	Travel	4334	002	Domestic Airfare
127	Expense	Travel	4334	003	International Airfare
128	Expense	Travel	4334	004	Passport, Visas & Other Charges
129	Expense	Travel	4334	005	Room Rent—Domestic
130	Expense	Travel	4334	006	Room Rent—International
131	Expense	Travel	4334	007	Halting Reimbursements
132	Expense	Travel	4334	008	Meals and Beverages
133	Expense	Travel	4334	009	Telephone Charges
134	Expense	Travel	4334	010	Other Travelling Expenses
135	Expense	Expenses	4402	000	Corporate social responsibility—CSR
136	Expense	Expenses	4422	000	Customer Seminars/Meetings
137	Expense	Expenses	4454	000	Internet Leased Line Charges
138	Expense	Expenses	4467	000	Landline Charges
139	Expense	Expenses	4468	000	Mobile Phone Charges

What the Finance

Sl No	Grouping	Sub Grouping	Main Account No	Sub Account No	GL Name
140	Expense	Expenses	4500	000	Other Stationery Expenses
141	Expense	Expenses	4508	000	Visiting Cards/Slips
142	Expense	Expenses	4511	000	Other Printing Expenses
143	Expense	Expenses	4544	000	Other IT Consumables
144	Expense	Professional fees	4567	000	Professional Fees
145	Expense	Professional fees	4567	001	Statutory Audit Fees
146	Expense	Professional fees	4567	002	Tax Audit Fees
147	Expense	Professional fees	4567	003	Audit—Out of pocket Expenses
148	Expense	Professional fees	4567	004	Legal Fees
149	Expense	Professional fees	4567	005	Secretarial Fees
150	Expense	Professional fees	4567	006	Other Professional Fees
151	Expense	Professional fees	4567	007	Out of Pocket Exp.
152	Expense	Repairs & Maintenance	4601	000	Repairs & Maintenance
153	Expense	Repairs & Maintenance	4601	001	Office Equipment Repairs and Maintenance
154	Expense	Repairs & Maintenance	4601	002	Computers Repairs and Maintenance
155	Expense	Repairs & Maintenance	4601	003	Vehicles Repairs and Maintenance
156	Expense	Repairs & Maintenance	4601	004	Furniture Rep. and Maintenance
157	Expense	Insurance	4627	000	Insurance
158	Expense	Insurance	4627	001	Travel Insurance
159	Expense	Insurance	4627	002	Other Insurance
160	Expense	Expenses	4636	000	Newspaper and Magazines
161	Expense	Taxes	4645	000	Other Rates and taxes
162	Expense	Expenses	4652	000	Bank Charges
163	Expense	Expenses	4659	000	Provision for Doubtful Debts
164	Expense	Rent	4704	000	Rentals

Sl No	Grouping	Sub Grouping	Main Account No	Sub Account No	GL Name
165	Expense	Rent	4704	001	Office Rentals
166	Expense	Rent	4704	002	Lease Equalisation
167	Expense	Maintenance	4716	000	Operational Maintenance
168	Expense	Maintenance	4716	001	Business Centre Charges
169	Expense	Maintenance	4716	002	Electricity Charges
170	Expense	Maintenance	4716	003	Water Charges
171	Expense	Maintenance	4716	004	Generator/Diesel Exp.
172	Expense	Amortisation	4742	000	Amortisation/Depreciation
173	Expense	Amortisation	4742	001	Depreciation—Office equipment
174	Expense	Amortisation	4742	002	Depreciation—Computers
175	Expense	Amortisation	4742	003	Depreciation—Vehicles

www.ingramcontent.com/pod-product-compliance
Lightning Source LLC
Chambersburg PA
CBHW020858180526
45163CB00007B/2553